The
OCTOBER SCENARIO

By

Captain Kevin D. Randle

UFO Abductions, Theories About Them
And a Prediction of When They Will Return

The OCTOBER SCENARIO

Library of Congress Cataloging-in-Publication Data
Randle, Kevin D, 1949-The October Scenario

Includes index:

1. Unidentified flying objects – Sightings and encounters. I. Title

TL 789.3.R34 1988 001.9'42 88-1669

ISBN-10: 0-934523-35-5
ISBN-13: 978-09334523-35-6

Library of Congress Catalog Card Number 88-1669

MIDDLE COAST
PUBLISHING

Iowa City Iowa

CONTENTS

Part I

A General Overview of October, 1973

INTRODUCTION

The University of Colorado study headed by Doctor Edward U. Condon, published in 1968, concluded that we could expect one visit by extraterrestrials every ten thousand years. Since that time, other scientists have echoed the claim that other intelligent life forms populate the universe and we can expect then to stop by once in a very great while. The only thing that none of them told us was when we should start counting.

Even the briefest survey of the fall of 1973 shows that it was a time of unparalleled UFO activity. Thousands of people saw them. Hundreds more witnessed them landing and dozens experienced sightings of the occupants riding in them, or were abducted for examination aboard them.

These then were not the high flying discs of the early 1950's or the close approaching craft of the mid-1960's, but vehicles that were touching down all over the United States and the Western Hemisphere. It was something that had been reported only sporadically prior to 1973. And it is something that might provide a clue into the nature of the UFO phenomena.

During the last ten years I have been talking to people who were involved with the October Scenario. As a former Air Force officer whose job put me into the middle of some of these things, I was able to bring a different perspective to the phenomena. I have met Charles Hickson. I have interviewed Leigh Proctor. I made an in depth study of the Roach affair and the Ramstead case. I have seen the files on the Llanca abduction. I talked with dozens of individuals who reported flying saucers during that time. In the midst of all this one thing became clear. This was not just another bunch of UFO sightings. This was something new and different.

During the years of investigation, I believe that I learned exactly what was different about the sightings of 1973. It wasn't any single thing, major or minor, but a string of ideas that can be gathered into a group that gives us the most exciting picture to date.

This was an investigation that could have been diverted in a number of places. Side tracked by the more exciting chapters of Ufology, or the more glamorous avenues in the UFO phenomena. Too many times, investigators are more interested in the photographs or the physical evidence, believing that proof of the UFO phenomena will appear in these cases. Too often, even the UFO experts shy away from the reports of occupants and abductions. It was this path that provided the final clues.

As we travel the paths that have been marked by the crews of the spacecraft it becomes apparent that there was a design. This was not the haphazard pattern that has emerged time and again. But to understand it, we must slowly move down the paths, examining each curve, each pothole, and each clue. Only then will we understand the force behind the October Scenario.

Kevin Randle

OCTOBER 1973:
A GENERAL OVERVIEW

The first indications that October 1973 was going to be different from the other UFO waves came a few weeks earlier. During August a man and his son were driving along a main New Hampshire highway when they saw a strange machine sitting in a nearby field and a tall humanoid standing beside it. Neither felt the urge to stop and examine the craft and they reported little additional detail.

Near the middle of September, a Sydney, North Carolina family reported seeing a creature with red glowing eyes, long hair, pointed ears, and a hook nose on a gray face. The creature seemed to limp and was missing a hand, but could leap fifty or sixty feet at a time. Later examination of the field where the alien had been seen revealed no footprints or other physical evidence.

Although that report fit no UFO category because a craft was not seen, it wasn't without substantiation. A radio disc jockey and a group of friends saw the same creature and fired five or six shots at it.

It was also during September that several Savannah, Georgia teenagers reported that ten black, hairy dogs came from a landed UFO and ran through a cemetery. Local authorities believed the report to be a hoax.

But, all that was little more than a prelude to October. It set the tone because nearly all the reports in October contained descriptions of occupants or of low flying discs. On the first of the month, three black men reported they saw a huge creature that walked mechanically. They also saw an egg-shaped UFO from which the,. imprints were later found.

Three days later a Simi Valley, California man, Gary Chopic, saw a

3

triangular shaped object hovering in a dust cloud near the Simi Freeway. In a clear bubble that was revolving on top of the UFO, the man saw a humanoid in a silvery wetsuit. When the creature saw Chopic, it leaped out of sight. The bubble began to rotate faster, seemed to disappear into the object, which emitted a whirring sound as a fog began to develop around the craft. Seconds later it disappeared. Chopic said that he didn't see it move, it just vanished. Chopic's report was the second received by Simi Valley authorities.

The next evening a retired school teacher and her daughter left El Centro, California for their home in San Diego when they saw a Greyhound Bus and several cars pulled to the side of the highway. Standing nearby were a number of people who were all watching something in the sky. The witnesses stopped their car and saw a single large, disc-shaped object surrounded by a glistening vapor. The object rose until it was about twelve hundred feet above the ground, turned and vanished, leaving a vapor to drift downwards. After a minute or two, that also disappeared. None of it reached the ground so that there were no samples of it available for analysis.

The following day the UFO's moved from California to Canada. A man and his wife, who wished not to be identified, claimed that early on the morning of October 6, they saw a bright spotlight bouncing over a field about a quarter of a mile from their house. The man assumed that it was the police chasing cattle rustlers since there had been a rash of such thefts in the area. Minutes after they first saw the light, it winked out and they thought no more about it.

The next day, the man was working behind the house when his wife came out to tell him that she could see dense black smoke coming from the location where they had seen the light. While watching the smoke, a "dome-shaped tent" of orange-yellow appeared about a quarter of a mile away. Both witnesses said that they didn't think the smoke had anything to do with the domed object.

After a few minutes, a "bulldozer" about a quarter of the size of the UFO came into view heading toward a spring. As it moved away, five "scouts", humanoids in bright, yellow colored clothes appeared and began running between the two objects. One of the witnesses said that she thought that they wore helmets but couldn't be sure because the grass was too tall and they were too far from her.

Both witnesses continued with their work which took them away from the general area, and when they returned, the object and the scouts were gone. They didn't search for evidence in the field at that time but wondered how the "men and their equipment" could have gotten out of the area without passing them and their house.

4

About noon, the witnesses' daughter returned and when she heard the story, she ran out to the area where the objects had been seen. She found flattened grass that led from the area to the spring. A few days later more flattened grass and a few broken bushes were found, leading to speculation that the men and their equipment had returned briefly.

For the next several days, the wave in the United States tapered. There were still UFO sightings, but they had gone back to the sky. There were bright lights streaking from east to west or north to south, glowing balls that hovered before darting away, and a few daylight UFO's seen in the distance. But, on October 11, it began to happen again. More UFO's were on the ground and more occupants were seen outside. In Tanner Williams, Alabama, a three year old boy told his mother that he had been playing with a nice monster that had grey, wrinkled skin and pointed ears. Had it not been for confirmation of that description a few days later, no one would have thought twice about the boy's playmate.

On the same day, but farther north in Connersville, Indiana, and just after four-thirty, Terry Eversole and his sister saw a disc-shaped object with a segmented compartment on the bottom, hovering over the trees near their house. They said that the object was silver with a dome on top and three green doors on the bottom. After several seconds it shot off toward the horizon and vanished.

Three hours later, also in Connersville, Indiana, Bill Tremper and nearly fifty others watched an oval shaped object with a pale yellow light on top and a segmented compartment on the bottom cross the sky until it was over a restricted government owned ammunition testing range. It hovered briefly and then gently settled to the ground. About thirty minutes later the object rose, hovered and disappeared in the northeast.

About that time, Randi Stevens, Joel Burns and three others saw a UFO hovering near Laurel, Indiana. They described the UFO as looking like two saucers joined at the rim with something on the bottom that appeared to be divided into three equal parts. The UFO hovered for about three minutes, until a truck driver who had been watching it got into the cab and blew the horn.

While the UFO's were hovering over Indiana, they were landing in Mississippi. About nine that night, two men walked into the Pascagoula sheriff's office and claimed that they had seen a strange object land. Several robot-like creatures came out of it, swooped toward them, grabbed them, and took them back to the UFO for some kind of examination. Within hours of making that report, Charles Hickson and Calvin Parker would be known across the country and all national UFO reporting would be centered on the small Mississippi town.

An hour and twenty minutes after Hickson and Parker began telling sheriff's deputies their story, Allen Robbins and his wife were trying to identify the strange object they had seen over Boulder, Colorado, minutes earlier. Robbins' wife saw the object first, a mass of lights approaching from high overhead, and called his attention to it. The slowly rotating object maintained a steady speed as it flew silently above them. Strung out on the bottom they could see a series of lights that divided into thirds.

While the press was tied up in Pascagoula and in Boulder, James Cline was awakened by barking dogs near Berea, Tennessee. A farm family saw the blinking lights of a UFO in the woods, and Cline saw a creature with a glowing white head cross the road about fifty feet in front of him. Tracks from both the creature and the UFO were found the next day.

On October 15, a cab driver on Interstate 90, between Gulfport and Biloxi, Mississippi, claimed that his cab was stalled by a blue UFO that landed in front of him. He then heard a tapping on his windshield and saw a "crab-like" claw thing and two shiny spots. There was some speculation that this was the second of the October abductions. Reports later claim that the cab driver confessed that he had made up the story, but this wasn't confirmed.

Then on Monday, October 16, Howard Moneypenny, a weather service specialist saw a bright light glowing in the distance. He pointed the UFO out to several others and a private pilot at the airport with him volunteered to give chase to the object, but gave up after several minutes, when he realized that he wasn't getting any closer. On his way back to the airfield, the airport manager warned the pilot that the object seemed to be chasing him. The UFO finally disappeared in the distance.

Also on the sixteenth, William and Donna Hatchett were traveling on an Oklahoma county road when they noticed a very bright light in the south. At first Hatchett thought that it was a farm security light on a pole, but it seemed to be moving with the truck and getting closer. As the UFO turned toward the truck and began descending, Donna begged her husband to stop for a moment.

When Hatchett stopped the truck, the object began hovering near the front of the pickup and above a nearby fence, and both Hatchett and his wife could hear or feel a penetrating, low pitched hum. There was a blinding white light coming from the object that Hatchett estimated to be the size of a Boeing 707 passenger jet. While Hatchett sat staring at the

6

UFO, his wife got out of the truck and moved toward the rear, as if to see better. Hatchett, now frightened, ordered her to return to the cab. She did as told, but got out twice more. With his wife back in the truck, Hatchett finally began driving away. As he did, the UFO moved off in the opposite direction, gaining altitude, but never much speed.

Both witnesses later reported that they felt that the creatures in the UFO knew everything that they were thinking. Donna Hatchett claimed that the flashing lights she saw as the craft pulled away from her reminded her of the lights on a computer. When they arrived in Drumright, Oklahoma, they reported the sighting to a policeman, but he was uninterested in it.

Researchers noted parallels between this case and the Hill abduction of 1961. Later researchers did not find evidence that the Hatchetts had been abducted, but it was an avenue that should have been examined before the idea was rejected.

And finally, on the sixteenth, two children reported a UFO with a pointed dome that made a buzzing sound. The older boy claimed that strange creatures offeredhim a chance to look inside the craft, but he was too frightened to do so. The boy's father said the family dog was quite agitated when he went into the backyard right after the incident.

Sightings didn't slow down the next day. There would be half a dozen reports involving occupants before the day was over. Later, researchers would realize that the seventeenth would mark the peak of the wave.

In Watauga, Tennessee a copper colored UFO hovered just about the ground while a tall creature with claw-like hands and wide, blinking eyes reached out to grab two children.

Another tall creature showed up in Falkville, Alabama where Police Chief Jeff Greenhaw photographed a "being" in a silvery suit after he was called to the area to check on a UFO report. Greenhaw stopped his car when he saw the creature and it moved slowly toward him. After a few moments it turned and began running. Greenhaw pursued it until his car spun off the road. Various investigators and UFO organizations labeled the case a hoax when NASA produced pictures of their metallic fire fighting suit that bore a strong resemblance to the creature in the Greenhaw photos. No one has proved that Greenhaw faked the pictures, and he has gained nothing from it if he did.

Small creatures in a cone-shaped object later landed on US Highway 29 in front of a car driven by Paul Brown forcing him to stop. As Brown got out of his car, two creatures dressed in silver suits and white gloves appeared. Seeing Brown, they returned to their craft, which took off immediately. Brown fired several shots from his revolver after it.

Back in Mississippi, another UFO landed on a highway blocking traffic. As one car approached the craft, its lights went out and the engine died. Occupants of the car saw a humanoid with a wide mouth, flipper feet, and webbing between the legs.

The third abduction of the month was reported near Loxley, Georgia. Clarence Patterson claimed his pickup truck was sucked into a huge, cigar shaped craft and that he was jerked out of the cab by several robot-like creatures who seemed to read his mind. He blacked out after that. The next thing he knew, he was on the highway driving at ninety miles an hour.

Perhaps the most important case came from Utah where a woman reported that she was taken from her house by several tiny creatures just before midnight. The beings who came from a UFO that landed in a secluded field near her home also took four of her children for examinations, however only the youngest remembers anything about the incident. The mother, believing that a prowler had been in her house, called the police. It would be more than two years before the details of the sighting would be learned.

On the eighteenth, there were more sightings of UFO's and the creatures flying them. Near Chatham, Virginia, two youths reported that they were chased by a white thing about three or four feet tall. The thing had a large head with no eyes and ran sideways. There were several other reports of UFO's made in the area.

Near Savannah, Georgia, a small silver creature was seen standing by the highway. Dozens of cars zipped passed it, but none of them stopped.

And finally, on the eighteenth, a patrolman for the Noblesville, Indiana police saw a cigar-shaped object just before midnight. Herchel Fueston had just arrived at the Morse Reservoir when he sighted the UFO in the northeast. He turned his spotlight toward it and it began moving to the southwest as its lights brightened.

The UFO flew over the reservoir and when it was directly overhead, Fueston thought that he could see a row of portholes. He couldn't see anything behind them and could see no markings on the craft. The UFO hovered briefly and then moved off after descending to treetop level.

The wave didn't taper much on the nineteenth. A woman driving near Ashburn, Georgia reported that her car engine died and she lost the power steering and brakes. As she coasted to a stop on the side of the road, a small man in metallic clothes appeared. The woman said the alien seemed to have a bubble head and rectangular eyes. It moved around the car as if inspecting it and then it vanished, much to the woman's relief.

Later that day, in Copeland, North Carolina, a farm couple found an oval UFO hovering near their home. There was a small humanoid in a gold, metallic jumpsuit moving near it. They observed no other detail, being afraid of both the craft and the creature that apparently came from it.

The last reported sighting on the eighteenth involved only a landed disc. Susan Ramstead said that her car engine was stalled when she approached a domed UFO sitting in a cornfield. Minutes later the craft shot skyward and vanished. Four years later it would be discovered there was much more to the report.

The next day, on October 20, a college student vanished on her way home for a few days. When she finally reappeared, on October 24, she claimed that she had been taken onboard an alien spacecraft and subjected to a series of long and painful stress tests. Investigations of the sighting progressed slowly because of the agitatnature of the young woman. Like the Utah case, the significance of the sight...4 wouldn't be fully realized for several years.

On the twenty-first, a mother and son in Ohio sighted a grey humanoid near a landed UFO. A later search of the area produced ground traces. Less than twenty hours later, on October 22, a series of sightings began in nearby Hartford City, Indiana, when Debbie Carney saw two creatures wearing silver suits cross the road in front of her car. She quickly drove past them. She didn't see any kind of a flying saucer.

Only fifteen minutes later, De Wayne Donathan and his wife were returning home when they saw a flash of light in the road in front of them. At first they thought they were about to hit a farm tractor and had only seen the reflector on the back of it, but as they approached, they saw two creatures jumping and leaping near the road. Donathan described their movements by saying they seemed to be dancing.

Donathan's wife, who was driving, panicked and jammed the accelerator to the floor as she swerved around the creatures. Donathan wasn't quite sure about whatever it was they had witnessed and convinced his wife to return by telling her that he thought they had seen kids playing some kind of prank. On the return trip, they found nothing unusual, although Donathan said that there had been some unidentified lights in the distance.

About two hours later, Gary Flatter, after hearing the Donathan's story, drove through the area looking for the two creatures. He noticed a high frequency whine and saw a line of small animals running across the road. An instant later he saw the creatures standing in a plowed field about seventy-five feet from him. After watching them watch the animals for a few minutes, Flatter turned his truck's spotlight on them and was nearly blinded by the

9

reflection from their suits. Flatter said that the creatures were about four feet tall, had egg-shaped heads and gas masks with tubes running to their chests. Shortly after flatter turned on his light, the creatures bounded out of sight. The next day footprints were found in the field.

After the Hartford City sightings, the wave declined rapidly. There were one or two occupant sightings on the twenty-third in Kentucky. A lone woman saw two small creatures and the object from which they came. A day later a North Carolina man's car engine was stalled by a low flying oval UFO. He reported to have seen a creature with blazing red eyes.

On October 28, the last of the October abductions took place. Dionisio Llanca was taken to a hospital near his home in Bahia Blanca, Argentina, where he complained of amnesia and loss of appetite. Doctors, using hypnotic regression, learned that Llanca had been picked up by two men and a woman from a UFO. Onboard the craft he had been subjected to a physical examination during which blood samples were taken. After 40 or 45 minutes he was put back on the ground and left alone.

Llanca's sighting closed out the occupant reports in October 1973, but the aliens flying them weren't done. On November 1, a series of sightings began in New Hampshire when Florence Dow heard a thump on her front porch and saw a motionless creature standing there wearing a black coat and wide brim hat pulled down over a face that looked as if it had been covered with masking tape.

The next night, Lyndia Morel saw a strange yellow light far in the distance as she drove to work. As she watched it, it seemed to come closer, until she could determine that it was spherical and covered with a honey comb, except for one oval window. Behind the window she could see the upper body of a creature with grey, wrinkled skin, and large, dark slanted eyes.

As she continued on her way, she felt drawn to the UFO and kept looking at it. She became frightened and wanted to get away from it. She pulled into a farm driveway, leaped from her car and ran to the back door so that she wouldn't be able to see the UFO. After several minutes of hammering on the door, she managed to awaken the house's occupant and convinced him that she wasn't crazy. While she was inside the house, the UFO vanished.

Two days later, Rex Snow and his wife were awakened just after midnight. Outside, Snow saw two small creatures wearing silver suits. They seemed to be gathering samples. Snow ordered his German shepard to attack, but it stopped far short of the creatures and ran back into the house, obviously afraid of them. Earlier that evening, Snow had seen a disc-shaped UFO.

After the New Hampshire series, the sighting reports dropped off dramatically. There were only six more occupant sightings in November and December of 1973. A woman in Louisiana reported sighting a three foot tall creature with red eyes. And three foot tall creature was seen in Greenville, South Carolina. Near Poteet, Texas a UFO hovered above a car and the tall, green occupants tried to stop the vehicle. In Oklahoma three men saw a creature with flashing lights on him. A fourth man reported the same creature and said that he had seen a glowing white light down a side road. In San Ardo, California, two men saw a spherical UFO and then saw two aluminum shapes. And in Canada a woman saw a four foot tall creatures with a round head, and with two glowing eyes.

There were at least five reports of abduction, rumors of six others, and several attempts, such as the Lyndia Morel sighting. There were also a number of other sightings where abduction might have taken place had the circumstances been slightly different. Or where it did take place but no one with the background to investigate the possibility was available. Hatchett and his wife could have been, or might have been, victims, had they not sped out of the area.

These correlations and conclusions, however, become more apparent as some of the abduction cases are examined in detail. And it doesn't completely stop with the October 1973 sightings. The similarities with certain other cases begins to build a file of evidence and abduction that becomes impressive. The real pattern, however, doesn't develop until in depth studies of the abductions are made. With that body of information, the October Scenario begins to take shape.

Part II
The Abductions

HICKSON-PARKER

The first reported abduction of the October wave took place near Pascagoula, Mississippi. Charles Hickson and Calvin Parker were fishing from an old pier on the west bank of the Pascagoula River when a blue light attracted their attention. At first, it was high overhead, but as they watched, it dropped toward the ground. Hickson said that it stopped only a few feet above the bayou, and it wasn't very far from them. Parker was badly frightened, his condition bordering on hysteria.

The light had turned into an object, and the object headed toward the river, hovering above it. Hickson recalled that he could hear a buzzing noise coming 11from it but there was no wind or blast like there would be from a jet engine. The UFO stopped moving not far away.

One end of the object seemed to open then and three creatures floated from it. Hickson described the creatures as about five feet tall, covered with wrinkled grey skin, long arms and lobster like claws for hands. The three creatures headed for Hickson and Parker. Hickson noticed that one of them seemed to be buzzing in much the same fashion as the object from which they came. The creatures separated slightly, one of them trying to pick up the now unconscious Parker, while two of them lifted Hickson, floating him toward the dimly glowing ship.

They went through a door that "seemed to appear" in the side of the oval. The interior of the ship was brightly lighted. The room was bare except for some kind of device at one end that Hickson described as looking like a big eye. All the time he was in the craft, he never touched any part of it. He seemed to float above the floor.

While he was on the ship, the creatures paid no attention to him. He tried to talk to them, but there was no response from them. After twenty or thirty minutes, he was taken back outside. Both men were floated to the river bank. Parker remembered nothing of the trip inside because he didn't regain consciousness until they had been returned to the bank.

Hickson didn't see the UFO disappear. He reported that he heard the buzzing and then it was gone. After the UFO vanished, Hickson tried to decide what to do, but fearing ridicule, was reluctant to talk to the authorities. And, he was busy trying to calm Parker who had regained consciousness, but who was still terrified.

Hickson's first reaction was that no one would ever believe him so it would be best not to tell anyone. Then he decided that someone in authority should be told, but he didn't know who. After several drinks in a local pub, an attempt to calm his nerves, he and Parker decided to talk to the local newspaper. If nothing else, they might be able to tell them who would be interested in the report.

The newspaper office was almost deserted. Hickson told the night man that he wanted to talk to a reporter, but was told that the reporters wouldn't return until the morning. Hickson decided that was too long to wait.

Next he tried Keesler Air Force Base. He received the standard Air Force reply which was that the Air Force no longer investigated UFO sightings. If Hickson felt a need to make a report to someone about the sighting, then maybe a local university or the sheriff might be interested.

Hickson opted for the sheriff. Once there, in the office, he told the sheriff that he didn't want any publicity, even though the first thing he had done was go to the newspaper office. His desire was not respected. By morning the whole country would know about the abduction. It's at this point that the story actually begins.

The leaders of the Aerial Phenomena Research Organization (APRO) Coral and Jim Lorenzen in Tucson, Arizona, heard about the case early the next morning. They scrambled, trying to find a psychologist who could go to Mississippi and begin the investigation. All three of their consultants in the field were busy. They turned to their Director of Research, James A. Harder, a civil engineer versed in hypnosis.

At the same time, J. Allen Hynek learned of the report. He had worked as

16

a consultant to the Air Force's Project Bluebook, and had called APRO to find out whether they thought the case worthy of investigation. Informed that APRO was sending a representative, Hynek made his plans to fly to Pascagoula.

By Saturday morning, the cast was assembled. Hickson and Parker met with Harder and Hynek in the offices of the J. Walker Shipbuilders Company. Hickson's attorney, Joe Colingo, Doctor Julius Bosco, Jack Walker, Deputy Sheriff Barney Mathis and police detective Thomas Huntly were all present.

At the onset both Hickson and Parker were afraid of hypnosis, their impressions of it having been formed by a dozen movies and television shows. Harder demonstrated the process on a couple of others and Hickson decided that it would be all right. The first session was little more than a dry run, getting Hickson used to hypnosis and ready for the regression that would take place later. Harder didn't quiz him on the sighting and gave him a post hypnotic suggestion that the headache Hickson had complained about would be relieved. Harder didn't ask about any of the things that had appeared in the newspapers and suggested that this session be ended quickly. He also suggested that the two men go home and try to rest.

The next day, the session was better. Harder was able to get right to the problem. He asked Hickson to describe, in detail, the event. Hickson reconfirmed that the object had come down behind them, was sixteen to eighteen feet long, and had a "trap door" in the back. The creatures floated out, grabbed them and floated them into the ship. After twenty or thirty minutes on the ship, the men were returned to the river bank.

Harder was impressed. After the session, he told APRO Headquarters that it would be nearly impossible for the men to simulate their feelings of terror while under hypnosis without some kind of outside stimulus. The terror both men displayed seemed to be quite real.

Newsmen gathered at the scene, asking both Hynek and Harder what they thought of the case. Harder said that he believed that something had happened to the two men and that it wasn't a terrestrial experience. Hynek didn't say that he believed that the men had seen something extraterrestrial, but did say that the men had had a very frightening experience. (There was also a persistent report that Hynek had fallen under the hypnosis as he watched the session, something that he later denied.)

The newsmen were not as reserved as Harder or Hynek. Headlines screamed that the "Scientists Believe UFO Story." A quick reading by the public and shabby research by the media gave the story an added note of credibility before the preliminaries were taken care of.

Late in October, after Harder and Hynek had had a chance to complete much of their research, a polygraph test was arranged in New Orleans. According to several sources, the test, which took nearly two and a half hours to complete, showed that Hickson had been telling the truth. More headlines were made. Newspapers claimed that the lie detector proved the story.

Philip J. Klass launched his own investigation into the affair. One of the first things he did was interview the polygraph operator. Klass felt that if the test was invalid, then he could label the case as a hoax since it was the lie detector test that gave an added note of respectability to the report.

Klass learned that the operator had only been working in the field for about a year and had not been certified by any of the reputable schools. Klass pointed out that Richard Arthur, director of the National Training Center of Lie Detection in New York City, said that the New Orleans operator who had examined Hickson had not finished his training. To Klass, this suggested that the exam had been rigged so that Hickson would pass.

Although the operator worked for a respected New Orleans detective agency,

Klass felt that the test proved nothing. He argued that making Hickson travel to New Orleans when there were certified operators closer suggested something unscrupulous. He suggested that another test, conducted on "neutral" territory by a certified, experienced operator would be the way to eliminate these doubts.

But Klass, Harder, and all the rest overlooked one important point. The lie detector test would only prove to a reasonable certainty that Hickson believed what he was saying. It would not prove that Hickson and Parker had been abducted. It would only prove that Hickson believed they had been.

And, there are ways to beat the test. According to experts, there is a small minority of people who can lie under the test conditions and the machine will not detect it. There are ways to prepare the test so that it can

18

be beaten. If this was not the case, there would be no need for juries in criminal matters. Just let the machine determine the truth.

It boils down to the fact that the lie detector test, used by one side to bolster its case is not that important. The test could have been rigged, Hickson could have beaten it, or he could have been telling the truth as he knew it. And that still wouldn't have answered the question of whether or not Hickson and Parker were abducted by aliens. That answer would have to be discovered through other methods and by comparing their case to the others that evolved in October 1973.

Two years later, the case took another convoluted turn at a UFO conference held in Fort Smith, Arkansas during October of 1975. Hickson was invited to tell his story, on the condition that he would submit to another lie detector test, arranged by the conference committee. This one would involve a police officer who had completed the school, who was certified, and who had worked with the machine for years. Hickson accepted the conditions and went to Fort Smith.

It wasn't until they were leaving for the police station that Hickson backed out. His attorney had advised against the new test. Klass saw this as an attempt to avoid having the truth told. Hickson said that any adverse publicity could hurt him financially. And no one pointed out that attorneys routinely advise clients against taking lie detector tests. The results are too open to too much interpretation. What one operator calls the truth, another might label a deception.

Again the controversy was stirred. Some criticized the organizers of the conference for wanting the test conducted at police headquarters. They claimed that the hostile surroundings could influence the results. They thought that a more convenient surrounding would have been better. The officer giving the test disagreed. He said part of the effectiveness of the test was to give it as he had given all the others. The austere background of the police station made the test more reliable.

For whatever the reasons, Hickson didn't submit to the test. He let the old one stand and has not tried to improve his case by letting a disinterested third party make the test.

While at the Fort Smith conference, I had a chance to talk to Hickson. He didn't stand there trying to be the center of attention as so many others had. He told his story again, adding to the details, correcting false information, and clarifying any misunderstandings that had developed in all the newspaper accounts.

It's some of those clarifications that have added to the controversy. For example, when Hickson appeared on one national TV show, he mentioned he was suffering from an eye injury from the bright lights in the UFO. It was the first mention of that. He had not said anything about it the day after the incident and hadn't told any of the doctors at Keesler Air Force Base about it. Philip Klass thought it strange that it had only manifested itself after several days.

The time of the sighting also changed. At first, Hickson said that they had first seen the UFO around seven in the evening. Later he thought it might have been as late as eight or possibly even nine. But Hickson later told me that he had never worn a watch. He had tried but it seemed that they all either lost time or gained time or stopped altogether. So he had no real way of knowing the time, except by the setting of the sun, which would have been fairly early in October.

It is the same with the dimensions of the ship. Originally Hickson said that the object was oval, about eight to ten feet wide and about eight feet high. Later he said that it was twenty feet long and later still he said twenty to thirty feet long.

All these points are minor. It could be Hickson, thinking about the sighting after it happened, realized that his original dimensions were small for what he was describing. Subconsciously he may have expanded them to fit what he thought would be right. It wouldn't be the first time that a witness had changed his story slightly to make it conform to what he believed to be the truth. Nor would it make that story untrue.

This is not to suggest that Hickson was lying. He may have honestly reported the dimensions. In a recent Iowa case, the young witness not only changed the shape of the ship after several interviews, in her later drawings she actually added humanoid figures to the "cockpit" because she had realized that there had to be a crew. She was not lying. Her subconscious was adding details that she knew had to be there. Her mind was playing tricks on her.

In October 1973, all this was not important. Hickson and Parker were the center of attention because their sighting had received publicity and they could remember details of the sighting. They could describe the

20

creatures from the UFO. Others, taken only days later, were not so lucky. Some would never consciously remember their sightings.

Pat Roach

The night Hickson and Parker were dragged into the flying saucer, they knew about it and so did the rest of the world. That statement is not as strange as it sounds. Others who had similar experiences didn't remember them and needed competent help to discover them. Although this incident happened within a week of the Hickson-Parker abduction, researchers wouldn't learn about it for two years. Only after hypnosis were members of the Roach family able to remember the UFO and its creatures. Consciously, they recalled a few things that provided clues about the night. They remembered a stranger in the house or a bright light shining into the living room from the open field outside the window, but they didn't remember seeing the craft or what happened on it. The only real exception was six year old Debbie. Her mother, Pat, when told of the spaceship, thought Debbie had seen too much TV. Only after Dr. Harder (APRO Director of Research) and I interviewed the victims at length did they seem to understand and accept what had happened. Unlike Hickson and Parker who said they wanted no publicity, but who are now world famous, Pat asked that her name be withheld to avoid the inevitable deluge of self styled investigators. Later, she reversed herself and her real name can now be revealed to the public.

On the night of October 16, Pat fell asleep on the couch in the living room. The kids were all in bed, except for the youngest who was asleep near Pat. Everything was quiet until just after midnight when Kent, the youngest, woke crying that he had seen a skeleton in the corner of the room. "Our cat

23

was screaming and I could hear the dog across the street barking. The noise woke the other children."

Reports of a prowler in the neighbor had been circulating and Pat was sure he had just been in her house. At 12:10 in the morning, October 17, she called the police. They arrived, questioned several of the family members, found nothing wrong, no prowler, and quickly left.

After the police were gone, Bonnie, the oldest girl said that there had been no prowler. "They were spacemen," she said. Pat then remembered the bright light earlier in the evening and that she had heard a "rustling noise" outside but she didn't remember much else.

Debbie, the youngest girl, only six in October, 1973, had a long story about a spaceship. "They didn't make me forget," she told her mother. "They told me not to tell anyone except those in my family." She described the ship, the creatures on it and the ones that had come into the house. Bonnie confirmed the description reluctantly.

Pat was convinced that Debbie had imagined many of the things that she had said. She granted that something strange had happened, but she didn't think it involved spacemen.

"Debbie told me about being on board the ship," Pat told me after several days of hypnosis and investigation. "The first few days after it, I didn't listen. It isn't something that happens to you or anyone you know. Not something that happens to real people."

For nearly two years the family did virtually nothing about that night. After discussing it among themselves, they had nowhere to go with it because they didn't know who to contact for help. After reading about the mysterious disappearances of people and the case of Dionisio Llanca in the UFO REPORT, Pat wrote to the magazine.

"All I wanted," she told me, "was to find out what happened. I didn't think that we had seen a UFO or had been in one, but there was that story told by Debbie. I just wanted to know."

The Roachs live in one of those small towns where everyone knows everyone else. I called the police to find out if there had been a prowler report and to get the date of the incident. They were very helpful. One of the police officers, Karl Zimmerman, knew Pat slightly and said that she seemed to be a very nice woman. She had not caused them any problems.

Pat doesn't really fit the normal pattern of the UFO reporters. Although she was separated from her husband, she had maintained a close friendship with him. Pat was working to complete her college education in the summer of 1975 and has since obtained her teaching certificate. She is one of the very few college educated people who has been involved in an abduction. During the course of our interviews with Pat, both Harder and I were impressed with her intelligence.

Others said much the same thing. They had known Pat for years, said that she was very nice and quite intelligent and not given to inventing stories. Several remembered the night when the prowler had been in the house. One of the closest friends remembered that Debbie had been violently sick just after the police left.

Everything that could be checked, showed that something had happened. There was a police report of a prowler. Others living in the area had seen him in the weeks before Pat's report. There was nothing left to do after I had checked out all these facts but call in someone who could use hypnotic regression to see if there wasn't anything that they couldn't consciously remember.

Coral Lorenzen of APRO called Harder and asked if he would be available for the sessions. He agreed to meet us in Lehi, Utah for a series of hypnotic sessions.

On July 8, 1975, we all met in Pat's house. She was anxious to find out about the night. Harder spent an hour talking to her, the children who were involved and listening to my preliminary conclusions. Just after noon, he felt that he had everything that he needed and suggested that we begin the real session.

He put Pat into a light trance, telling her to relax, "...to get that feeling of concentration...that feeling that you had that day. And now you remember that you woke up. You can tell us about it now. What was the feeling that you had?"

"I'm surprised." Pat spoke quietly and clearly. It was obvious that she wanted to remember.

"You felt surprised? Did you wake up then?" asked Harder.

"It was a bright light...when I woke, Kent wasn't with me. You know, I remember two figures standing over me."

That confirmed, right in the beginning, that someone or something had actually been in the house. It was important that she mentioned two figures because the girls had only talked about one that had stood in the corner. It meant that she had not taken the details from her conscious memory. With her under hypnosis, we had hoped to add to those details.

"What happened then?" asked Harder. "You can get that memory back. Just feel yourself being there." Harder moved the tape recorder so that the mike was in front of Pat.

"I remember looking up...They're bright and skinny. Whatever they were, they're skinny...they're dressed up like people that would be in the service."

"What gave you that idea?"

"Their uniforms." The answers were coming slowly. We had known about the creatures in the house, but we were now moving into new territory. These memories were upsetting Pat. The strain was evident on her face and in her voice.

"It looked like they're organized. I don't want to go with them." Pat's forehead creased and she began to perspire. "My arms ache," she said. She massaged her upper arm briefly, giving us the impression that she had been grabbed there by the aliens.

"I'm worried about my kids," she said without prompting. "Everyone is in

26

the room. No. Not everyone."

Harder said, "Let's go around the room and see who is there. You can see them. Just get that feeling. Just picture who was there."

"Bonnie is standing there. Debbie is there and I can't see Kent. I have the feeling that someone is carrying him but I don't see how that could be. They're holding him. They have us all."

"Was Shawn there?" Shawn was one of Pat's older sons.

"I see Shawn. It's a group and the one in the corner comes closer. He is standing by us." Pat was becoming frightened and then added quickly, "I don't remember what happened."

Harder had to reinforce the hypnotic trance. "You can remember," he told her. "You can tell us what happened. Were you told that you wouldn't remember?"

"They have a machine that they carry," Pat said. Bonnie later described it as the size of a briefcase that stood on three short legs. Bonnie had not been told that her mother had mentioned a small device but remembered it independently. Neither knew what the machine was for, only that it was left in the living room until the aliens left after the Roachs had been returned.

Pat continued to describe the scene in the living room. "They're very business-like and they hurt my arms because I don't want to go anywhere." She stopped for a moment and we could see that she was becoming more frightened as she remembered more about that night.

"They grasp me on each side of my arms. I can see my children fighting now."

Harder tried to soothe her, to reassure her that everything was fine. "They're going to be all right. It may be a little bit frightening but you can remember. You were all right afterwards, so it's all right to remember."

"I see a bright room. A big, bright room u.1d they're standing around." She had jumped from the living room to the interior of the ship as if the trip

27

from the house had frightened her and she didn't want to talk about it.

"How many can you see?"

"Four or five. All have uniforms. I wonder if I really see this...or if it's my imagination." Pat hesitated. She might have been listening. "They're not as nice as they wanted me to think. They were cold blooded but they didn't want me to know it.

"Is there something that happened that made you think they were cold blooded?" "They treated me like a guinea pig." Pat was more angry than frightened now. "They really didn't care about people as people."

Harder tried to direct the questioning to another area. Pat was becoming upset talking about the aliens. "What was the shape of the room?" he asked her.

"Round. I can see out at the stars. Not through the top but on the side, toward the top."

"Is it clear?"

"No. It's as if you could see the stars. It looked like a lot of technology. It's all machines and buttons."

"What kind of machines? Did they look like typewriters? Computers?"

"They looked like computers. They had wavy lines going through them. That's all I remember now."

"Is there something that you think would be frightening to remember?" Harder asked her again.

"Yes. I know there is."

Harder glanced at me and frowned. "You know, you got out of this perfectly safe...is there something you think that..."

"I don't remember being examined but I know I was."

That stumped us for a moment. Harder stopped his questioning and looked at me and then out the door. For the next fifteen minutes, he went over many of the points that Pat had already told us. He pushed briefly, trying to get at the examination. Pat outlined what happened but she became frightened. The answers were sometimes slow and disjointed. She really didn't want to remember the examination. Harder pushed again, trying to reinforce his hypnotic control. "It is possible that you were persuaded that you might not remember but you really can if you want to."

"I know I can but I don't want to remember it now."

"Is it because it is too frightening?"

"I was upset."

"You didn't like their attitude." It was really a question.

"No." Pat just sat for a moment. She raised her hand and hit the tape recorder. Her face wrinkled and she spoke softly, slowly. "I had to do what they wanted me to do. I didn't know what was happening to my children. I don't see them like I thought they were."

Momentarily confused, Harder asked, "You see them, the aliens, differently now than you thought you saw them?"

"I didn't see them before but my children had described them."

For the next few minutes, Harder tried to build a description of the aliens. They were slightly over four feet tall and very thin. Their eyes were very big and slanted. Their arms were long and ended in claws with an opposable thumb. They seemed to be wearing fluorescent clothes with a Sam Browne belt and Pat thought that they were wearing gloves.

The session continued for a few more minutes but we were covering the same ground over and over again. Pat described how they were "floated back to the house," and that Kent woke, screaming about the skeleton. Pat woke and called the neighbors who called the police. The rest of the night was a jumble of running out of the house, knowing that something strange had happened but not what. Pat and the kids were afraid to stay in the house and she took them to the neighbors for the rest of the night.

Harder was now trying to calm Pat, explaining that she should try to remember so that she could reassure the children. "They'll want to know and you should remember so that you can tell them," he said quietly. He switched tracks again and said, "What kind of information do you think they wanted?"

"They wanted to know how our minds work. They wanted it to give them certain information that they don't know yet."

"It would be very helpful for me to know, as a scientist, what kinds of things they were looking for."

"How we think. How we feel. Our emotions."

"That's interesting," said Harder. "Do you think it makes them interesting?"

"NO! I don't like what they want." She was obviously angry again. Angry and frustrated.

"You thought you were being intruded upon?"

"Yes. They didn't care because they don't have an understanding of emotions like ours."

Pat suddenly came out of the trance and for a moment, she sat quietly rubbing her eyes. It was no longer a mystery but it was not the glamorous experience that she had thought. It was something that was frightening. We discussed what she had said and she remembered a few additional details. We had given her no hypnotic command to forget so the experience was fresh, as if it had happened only days before. She now knew that Kent had not been onboard the spacecraft, but that three of the children had been.

One other fact came out after the session. Pat, and later Bonnie, mentioned a series of pin pricks, on their upper arms. Pat thought that the three tiny holes, arranged in an inverted triangle had been done by the aliens and she was very upset by them, almost afraid to look at them. When they faded a

30

few days later, she was quite relieved. One of the neighbors remembered seeing the marks on both Pat's and Bonnie's arms but Pat brushed her off. After all, the "wounds" were so minor and no one seemed to be hurt by them. Pat said that she had considered seeing a doctor but it seemed to be too much trouble.

Before we started with Bonnie, I had a chance to discuss Pat's session with Harder. I had been involved with the investigation for nearly six weeks and was afraid that I was getting too close to see it clearly. I wanted an outside opinion. I asked Harder what his first impressions were.

"It's a little early to be sure but it seems to be good. There are several things I want to check. We'll have to wait to see what the others have to say."

The next session was a disaster. Bonnie, a high school student in the summer of 1975, was afraid of what she might remember and was frightened of hypnosis. Harder tried to relax her and she began to slip into a light trance. But, the distractions were too great and she woke before we had a chance to probe the case. We tried again, but it was too noisy. Again she woke, remembering virtually nothing.

We decided that it might be best to try again after dinner. We arranged for Pat, Bonnie and Debbie to meet us in the nearby Holiday Inn. There, we could control the conditions better and had a chance of keeping Bonnie in a trance. At least, we thought we did.

Bonnie slipped into the trance faster than she had during the afternoon. She went under easily and Harder asked a few questions that didn't pertain to the UFO. Bonnie didn't react but did remain hypnotized. As the questioning turned toward the aliens, Bonnie's forehead creased and she woke. We tried once more but the results were the same.

Debbie was more willing to cooperate. Although she was only six when this happened, she has an amazing I.Q. She grasps things quickly, as quickly as some high school students, and yet hasn't been known to tell tales. She is small for her age so in 1973, she looked like she was four. That might be why the aliens left her memory intact. She too, was very interested in all that had happened. After the police left, she had told her mother she remembered the aliens. She described the one who had stood in the corner. She talked about the "line" of people she had seen waiting to "get on the machine."

Earlier I had asked her to talk about all she could remember. There were many things but it had been two years and she had forgotten a lot. She did remember seeing an "Indian girl" on the saucer. I asked how she knew the girl was an Indian.

"She was dark and had on a long dress."

"You said that they talked to you."

"They thought at me with their heads."

"Do you remember what they said?"

"The one that stood in the corner asked my name. And he said that I wouldn't be sick anymore."

Pat had said that Debbie had been very sick before the aliens arrived and theyhad done something to her or for her. The sickness was gone after the aliens left.

Debbie told me that she had seen several people standing in a line, waiting to get on "the machine." She didn't know what the machine was or what it did, but said that it seemed to be a floating table with all kinds of dials on it. In the line, she could see her sister, Bonnie, and she recognized two young neighbor boys. It meant that not only members of the Roach family were involved but that the aliens had taken quite a few people onto their spacecraft. We were able to get the names of all those she had seen.

Things were beginning to look bad, however. We had not been able to actually confirm anything. All we had was Pat's word about the incident. Everything that we had learned from interviewing the family members were things that Pat had already described to us with a couple of minor exceptions. They could have picked up the story listening to their mother.

32

There were little things that were coming out, but the point of origin for the whole story seemed to be Pat. At one point or another, Pat talked about everything seen in the house and out. She mentioned the alien in the corner to us first under hypnosis, but then Debbie mentioned it. Was that confirmation, or something that she had somehow gotten from her mother somehow in the last two years? If one of the girls would talk to us under hypnosis and tell us something about the experience that Pat hadn't witnessed, we would have a stronger case. We had to give up for the evening but hoped for something more the next day.

We arrived early the next morning. Debbie met us and while we waited for Pat, I talked to her again. We talked about everything and I slipped a few questions about the UFO into the discussion. I wanted to know which alien had told her that she wouldn't be sick anymore.

"The one in the house," she said, rather put out that I had forgotten. "You mean the one in the corner?"

"No. The other one."

"You saw more than one in the house?"

"There was one in the corner and the one who stood near the couch."

Here, at last, was some confirmation. No one had mentioned more than one in the house until Pat had said it under hypnosis and we tried to make sure that no one told the girls about it. The point wasn't major, and still suffered from the fact that Pat had mentioned it while under hypnosis the day before, but it was a fact no one had spoken about out loud.

I tried a new tack but it went nowhere. It seemed that the more I questioned her, the less she remembered. I had the impression that she had been programmed to forget if anyone outside the family began to press her about the experience.

Pat arrived and we decided to try another session with her. There were still many interesting things to pursue. After a good night's sleep, Pat was ready to try to tell us more about the examination.

Harder put her into a deep trance, much deeper than the one he had used the day before. He tried to reinforce our strength. He spoke softly and in a monotone. (I listened carefully, but remembering what I had heard about Hynek who had concentrated too fully on the progress, I kept looking around. I didn't want to be accidentally hypnotized.)

"And as time goes on," Harder said in his quiet voice, "that part of your mind is going to be stronger and stronger and you're going to resist the original suggestion of what you should forget. Now you can start to talk and tell me what was the first impression you got from them."

"They wanted me to go with them."

"Did you go willingly?"

"I went at first." The craft wasn't far from the house, less than fifty yards away. It hovered over a small, tree-lined pasture, effectively hidden from sight. They were floated toward a door or hatch in the side of it. The aliens apparently weren't bothered by walking into a house and they even invaded the bedrooms to get Bonnie, Debbie and Shawn.

Pat had been silent for a few minutes now. Harder tried to strengthen his control. "It's hard for you to remember. It's very disturbing but you can still remember. You got out all right and Debbie was much better afterwards. Let's just get that feeling of being there and remember."

"They put me on a table and they hooked me up on one leg and one arm." She hesitated and then added angrily, "I didn't like their examination."

"Was it like a G-Y-N exam?"

"That's part of don't like what they do with my head."

"What are they doing?"

"Taking my thoughts."

That stopped us. Harder looked at me and frowned. He checked what she had said by asking, "They were taking your thoughts?"

34

Pat sighed and trembled slightly. "Yes."

"How did you know?"

"I could feel it." She said that softly. Then, angrily, "They don't have the right to take them."

"Of course they don't," said Harder trying to calm her. "What kind of things do they do to take your thoughts?"

"They put a needle in and they take my mind, my thoughts." She spoke so quietly that we could barely hear her.

"Where was the needle?"

"I can see it coming toward me. I don't know where it goes."

"Yes! You do!" said Harder, almost demanding an answer from her. "To the front of me. I don't know."

"Yes," he said again. "You do remember. You're strong enough and your will power can make you remember." Harder slipped into a rhythmic and soothing voice. He was forcing her into a deeper trance where the alien control would be weaker, easier to break. "It would be good to know what they did," he told her. "I'd better not."

"You see," he told her, "that was two years ago and you know we're just trying to find out. Nothing serious happened. They didn't understand the will power you had."

"I hope they all crash." She said it quickly and we weren't sure she had said it. "What was that?"

"I hope they all crash."

Suddenly we leaped over a span of time and Pat said, "I'm getting dressed. They don't know."

Harder went along with her. "Don't know what?"

35

"They don't know how we humans are. I called them stupid." Pat laughed as she remembered that.

"What did they say to that?"

"They weren't angry. They just do what they want to. The man was a regular man."

We weren't ready for that. "What? What was that? You thought there was a regular human being with them?"

"Yes."

"Was he taller? Bigger?"

"Yes. He was bald."

"Was he the one who did the examining?"

"He helped."

We wondered if this wasn't a trick her imagination was playing on her. She might believe that there was a human "doctor" with the aliens because of the exam that was performed. Somehow believing that a human examined her made it easier for her to cope with. Or maybe there was a human with the aliens.

"Did you clearly distinguish him from the others?" Harder asked her. "How did you know that he was human?"

She described his eyes. Regular human eyes. Then she began talking about the needles that were pushed into her and some of the things that the aliens had done. She told us that she was standing on a cliff, watching the waves roll slowly to shore. Her voice became quiet and monotonous. The sea scene and the repetition suggested that she was being hypnotized by the aliens. Now she remembered what they had asked.

"What I love. What I hate. What animals I like. They asked about my family. They manipulated me."

"Why did you think that?"

"I had no choice."

"What kind of information do you think they wanted?"

"They need us."

"What?"

"I don't know why they need us."

We waited a moment but Pat remained silent. Finally she said, "They're very intent. They need information quickly. I don't know if it's my imagination but they limit time."

That was confusing. Harder asked her to say it again.

"They limit time and we don't."

"What gave you the impression that they had a limited amount of time?"

Pat interrupted him. "Not amount of time. I don't know what it means. Just that they limit time."

For a few minutes she described the feelings that were building. We wanted to know if they had her in hypnosis but she didn't know. We asked if it was similar to the feeling that she had now and she said, "That's why I don't like this."

The exam on the craft ended and she remembered putting on her clothes. The aliens didn't help but stood waiting. Pat was becoming concerned about her children. She asked where they were and when the aliens didn't say anything, Pat was afraid that they had been hurt. She started to cry and asked for her children. Harder told her it was all right and her children were safe. She came out of the trance on her own.

She calmed down quickly and wanted to talk about the experience. She described the human in greater detail. He was about 55 and had a fringe of slightly gray hair around his head. He wore glasses, was dressed in black and had his hand in a rubber glove. Pat said that he had been nice but had tried to fool her into believing that he let her ride in the ship.

Pat finally excused herself and went into another room. When she was gone, Harder said that he had been worried because Pat had failed to display any real emotion during the first sessions. For Harder, Pat's emotions in the last hour had added a dimension of realism to the story. He was becoming convinced that Pat and her family had been on a flying saucer.

Bonnie agreed to try another session. She slipped into the trance in seconds and Harder questioned her about her birthdays. When he felt that she was into a deep state of hypnosis, he asked about the night the aliens were there. Bonnie woke up as he asked the question.

At first we hadn't noticed, but she always woke up as he asked the questions about the aliens. It suggested that the experience was too frightening and that her mind was protecting her or that a very strong block had been placed there by the aliens. We decided that we had to try something completely different.

Harder put her under again and told her that we wouldn't ask any questions. All she had to do was concentrate on remembering what had happened. If she wanted to talk to us, all she had to do was lift her hand, but we wouldn't ask any questions unless she indicated she wanted to answer them. The decision was hers.

After a few minutes, Bonnie awoke again but this time she remembered more about the experience and was able to describe the aliens and the inside of the ship. Many of the things she said confirmed what Pat had already told us. This was the breakthrough that we had been looking for and we now had the story from two separate points of view. Not a single one that sounded as if one person had originated it and communicated it to another person. A separate and different point of view. Different enough to suggest they were telling the truth.

In the case of Barney and Betty Hill, a New Hampshire couple who claimed they were abducted in the early sixties, Barney never added details that hadn't already been mentioned by Betty. He merely described the same scenes in less detail. That led some researchers to suggest that he had, somehow, learned the story from Betty. We no longer had that problem.

That evening we arranged for the final sessions with Pat and Bonnie because we had the best luck with them and we felt that we had gotten everything we could from Shawn and Debbie. We hoped that we would be able to confirm many of the things that Pat had told us and we wanted her to draw the aliens while she was under hypnosis.

Both were put into hypnosis at the same time. Bonnie was left to concentrate on only the ship and what was happening to her while Pat was given a pen and paper and asked to draw an alien. She sat on the couch, apparently looking at something. She stared at it for several minutes and then began to draw. It seemed that she was studying a model that we couldn't see. The picture looked like her descriptions but it was vastly more detailed.

For a few minutes we questioned Pat. She again described the human who worked with the aliens. She told us about the interior of the craft. She saw a "clock with a lot of hands. It's going around but I can't see too well." Later she told us that she hadn't been wearing her glasses so that was why she hadn't been able to see any printing on the "clock."

Harder started his tape recorder. "What else do you see?"

"Glass cases."

"What's in them?" I held my breath because I thought they were going to be specimen cases.

"They're on the wall and they look like they have colored liquid in them. I can't see too clearly without my glasses and it's so bright. Let me get down."

Pat described being wiped with a cloth and then being given her clothes. No one helped her until they floated her back to her house. She was worried about her children and began to cry. She woke up quickly, before we were ready. Now she remembered the needle and thought that it had been pushed into her stomach. That led to several frightening conclusions including the possibility that the aliens were, and are, breeding humans.

Bonnie woke and she remembered being on the craft. She was standing near a wall and could see the aliens around a table that floated. Her mother was on the table and Bonnie hesitated to say it, but her mother had no clothes. She didn't watch the examination too closely because she was scared. Then she dropped the bomb.

"I can see a human with them."

She went on to say, "He was taller and he had an ear like a human."

She then took the paper and drew the scene as she remembered it. It agreed with what Pat had said. The numbers and positions were all correct, just shown from a different angle. We quizzed her on it, but there was nothing new being added.

After Bonnie and Pat left, Harder and I discussed the case in detail. It matched several other reports, some of which hadn't received any wide circulation and only someone who studied the phenomena would be familiar with all those cases. There was no way Pat and her children could have had the knowledge to fake the story.

There were many things in the story that added to the credibility. One was the fact that most of the story came out under hypnosis. While the use of hypnosis doesn't necessarily provide a path to the truth, and the subject can lie, Pat's emotions suggested that she was telling the truth as she knew it. Her emotions were genuine and her statements under hypnosis, the worrying about her children, are consistent with the emotions one would expect.

Pat's descriptions of the alien's examination of her and the questions they asked were also very interesting. It appeared, from what Pat told us, that the creatures were building some kind of a psychological profile of humans. Pat had said that they didn't understand how we were or our emotions and some of their actions proved that. They didn't seem to worry about the psychological damage or problems that they might be creating. They were only interested in getting their information as quickly and quietly as possible.

The human working with them is something that has been reported before, though not widely, but it is still frightening. We're not sure what it means. He might have been someone who was working with the aliens for his own personal gain, he might have been under the influence of "mind control" or he might have been some kind of test tube experiment that required some kind of additional training, hence Pat's report that they were studying our emotions.

After the interviews with Pat, I continued the investigation. The only hitch in the story, the only negative aspect I found was the Chief of Police in the small community near Pat's home. He said that he thought "Pat is a nut." But then, his description of a nut was anyone who receives a traffic ticket and has the guts to protest it. He had a long list of local "nuts."

One of the major problems had been pinning down the time of the sighting. Pat had said that she had seen her clock, inside the house, that showed the time as five minutes after twelve. Bonnie insisted that everything had taken place at one o'clock. And then I realized that the near-sighted Bonnie glancing at the clock after the frightening experience might mis-read it and five after twelve looks like one o'clock. That was the kind of detail that hoaxers would not make up. A little thing that underscored the veracity of the report.

Before Harder and I separated to return home, I asked him how he felt. He said, "At first I was skeptical because of the lack of emotion. But that has been taken care of. Pat was certainly bothered by the last two sessions. Couple that with the information from a couple of other recent sightings and it becomes an outstanding case."

SUSAN RAMSTEAD

Hickson and Parker remembered their sighting from the very beginning. Pat Roach only remembered something strange although her daughters insisted that "spacemen" had been in the house. Susan Ramstead remembered nothing except a close encounter with a landed, brightly glowing disc. She remembered seeing it on the ground and then seeing it vanish into the distance, but she couldn't remember it taking off. That was the first clue. But there were others.

It was late in 1977 when I first talked to Susan Ramstead. She was a 35 year old business woman who worked for a local corporation. She had graduated from college with a degree in business administration and was putting that degree to good use. Like many UFO witnesses, especially those who hold relatively responsible positions in corporations, she was reluctant to talk about flying saucers. But after I spoke to a local service organization about some of the cases I had worked on, she came forward to tell me about her experience.

She said that she had left her apartment early in the evening in October 1973. She couldn't remember the exact date but she knew it was in October because she had just heard about the two men in Mississippi (Hickson and Parker). She planned to attend a special business seminar that was being held in a nearby community. Although it was fairly early, there was almost no other traffic on the highway. She couldn't remember for certain, but she thought the night was overcast. She remembered looking for the moon and stars but didn't remember seeing them.

Susan had just passed the halfway mark when she noticed a bright light over the next hill that was similar to the headlights of an oncoming car. She later said that she thought the lights were a little bright, but that she wasn't particularly interested in them. She dimmed her own lights, but when she crested the hill, it wasn't a car that she saw.

Below her, sitting in the remains of a cornfield, was a disc shaped object. She slowed slightly, wondering if she was actually seeing one of the UFO's that everyone had been talking about. She picked up the microphone of her CB radio and tried to call her husband who asked her to describe the craft.

"I told him that it was about twenty-five or thirty feet in diameter, had a slight dome on top and was glowing with a bright blue light. I first thought that it was sitting in the field, but as I approached, I saw that it was hovering about three feet high."

Her husband was getting excited and asked if she had her camera, but she had left home without it, one of the few times that she had gone out without it. He asked if there were any creatures around it, but the signal from the CB began to break up. The air seemed filled with static. Susan tried to tell her husband what was happening, but couldn't get through to him.

"I watched the thing for a few moments. I think I had taken my foot off the gas so that I was slowing down. I pulled to the side of the road. I don't remember doing that," she told me. "But I must have because I suddenly realized that I was sitting there watching the craft take off. I hadn't seen it lift. It was suddenly in the air high overhead. Then it turned to the south and disappeared in a couple of seconds."

The small crowd from my lecture pressed forward, each with his or her own experience or with another question. I watched Susan Ramstead back away and listen. When the group thinned, I asked if I could talk to her further about her sighting. I mentioned that it came during a time of great UFO activity and since she saw it on the ground, I would like to know about it. She was reluctant to talk further about it. She said that she'd rather forget it now, but finally consented to a formal interview.

I arrived at their house on a sunny Saturday afternoon. (They had long since abandoned their apartment in favor of a house.) Susan met me at the door, introduced her husband, John, and invited me into the living room. We sat down and talked briefly. She said that she now had the date of the sighting because she had managed to find a copy of the program from the seminar. The date was at the top. October 19, 1973.

I asked a few questions that UFO investigators always have to ask about smoke, haze, sound and colors, using a copy of a fairly standard form. Then I asked the jackpot question. It was something that no one had bothered with until then. I asked, "How long was it in sight?"

She said, "About five minutes. Maybe a little longer. I can't be sure because I didn't look at my watch."

Her husband broke in then. He said, "No, it was closer to twenty minutes. I looked at the time right after I lost contact and then noted it when I finally raised you. You said that it had just left."

There was a moment of stunned silence. I immediately realized that I had stumbled onto something more significant than a close encounter with a landed UFO. Here was a time discrepancy, the red flag of an abduction case.

Susan argued with her husband. She was sure that the craft hadn't been in sight more than five minutes. Ten at the very most.

I stopped them by asking, "Would you be willing to undergo hypnosis?"

For a moment Susan said nothing. She glanced at her husband and finally said, "If John can be there too."

I said that I could see no problem with that. We discussed it further. I tried to convince them that I wanted to use hypnosis to get at the details. We could, under hypnosis, get a better idea of exactly what had happened, how long the craft had been in front of her, and possibly retrieve a few long forgotten details. The last thing I wanted to do was suggest that she might have been abducted. She hadn't said a word about it, and later, I didn't want to be accused of originating the idea. I tried to convince her that the hypnosis was a routine we used often in close encounter cases.

We scheduled another session for the next Saturday. I would call if I could find a hypnotist, something that I hadn't been bothered with before. APRO had provided Harder for the Roach case, but this seemed to be such a long shot that I didn't want to waste APRO's limited resources and I found it hard to believe that the Ramsteads could have discussed the sighting with each other and never noticed the time discrepancy.

"And yes," she explained in answer to another question, she had been late to the seminar.

My first task was to find a local man or woman with the proper certificates and credentials. Any fair sized city will have a number of people versed in hypnosis advertising to help the overweight, help the smoker quit, and a variety of other services. A portion of these will have been trained in reputable schools and will understand the workings of hypnosis. I called four of them before I found one who would be willing to work with me on the investigation, and who seemed to have a mind open enough to at least accept the idea that what I was suggesting was within the realm of possibility.

This time we met in the home of the hypnotist. She had suggested that the unfamiliar surroundings, while not really distracting from the hypnosis, might give us a better perspective for the case. No one seemed inclined to argue.

The first attempt at hypnosis presented no problem; Susan Ramstead was a good subject. She slipped into the trance easily. The hypnosis regressed her to a birthday party when she was ten, and then woke her. This was standard procedure to introduce the subject to hypnosis while avoiding the experience that we were interested in because it was felt it might be traumatic, especially if I was right.

46

The second attempt, about thirty minutes later, went off without a hitch. Susan slipped into the trance easily. The hypnotist reinforced it gently, telling her to "...put herself back, back to the night when she saw something strange. To let the feelings and impressions come slowly and easily. To just get the feeling of being there."

"That's the strangest thing I've ever seen," said Susan. "It's just sitting there."

The hypnotist looked at me and said to Susan, "You know Kevin. He's right here and he's going to talk to you. You will be able to hear only his voice and mine."

I slid my chair closer to the couch, switched on my Sony tape recorder and asked, "What are you seeing?"

"Something strange. Blue. It looks like one of those flying saucers but that can't be. They don't exist."

"What's the flying saucer doing?"

"It's sitting in a cornfield. No, not sitting. Hovering, I guess. Just above the ground. It doesn't seem to be spinning."

"What are you doing?"

"I'm slowing down. I don't want to get too close to it. I think about the CB and wonder if I can get my husband. I know that he would be interested."

"Then what happened?" I realized that my questions were nothing Earth shattering, but I didn't want to be accused of leading the witness. After several people had heard the tapes we made with Pat Roach, or had read the transcripts, they had said that Harder had asked a number of very leading questions.

Susan went on. "I picked up the microphone and called John. At first, he didn't answer."

John Ramstead interrupted. "Whenever Sue is out at night like that, I leave

47

the set on in case she needs to contact me. I was in the other room when she called. I didn't hear her at first."

Susan ignored the interruption because she couldn't hear his voice (The hypnotist had, after all, told her she would hear nothing but my voice and hers). "I told him what I was seeing. He wanted to know if I had my camera but I didn't. I didn't think I would see anything worth photographing at the seminar."

"Go on," I said. "What happened next?"

"I talked to John for a few moments and then the radio just filled with static and quit working. My headlights dimmed and the car stops. I steer for the shoulder of the road, fighting the wheel because it's hard to turn it. I try to restart my car but the engine wouldn't even turn over. I'm pissed because John had said that we should buy the radios in case one of us gets stranded and now the radio won't work."

"And then?"

Susan's forehead creased and she began to perspire, the sweat beading on her forehead and upper lip. "Nothing," she said. "I can see nothing."

I remembered how Harder had handled similar problems in the Roach case a couple of years earlier, and said, "You can remember. You got out of the situation all right. If you think back, you can remember. What are you seeing now?"

"They're around the car. Four or five of them. Five. Standing there looking in the windows at me. I pick up the microphone and scream into it, but John wouldn't answer."

John Ramstead slumped into his chair and said, "Oh, God!"

I shot him a look. The blood had drained from his face. I asked, "What do they look like? What are they doing?"

"I can only see part of them. They seem to be only about five feet tall. The one by the door has a pasty white face and huge eyes that are elongated. I

48

can't see a nose or a mouth. Just a couple of holes where the nose should be and a line for the mouth. I keep looking from him to the one in front of the car.

"They're standing there looking at me, as if they can't figure out how to open the doors. I push the lock down on my side and lean across the seat to push down the other lock. For a moment we are all just standing and sitting around looking at each other. That's all I remember."

At this point it was obvious that Susan was frightened. I decided to jump ahead and find out if she was taken on board or if the creatures just studied her in the car for a few minutes. I said, "You are all right. They can't hurt you. You're out of the car? What happened after you were out of the car?" (I realized it was a leading question, but Susan had been reluctant to talk about the situation.)

"I'm inside. Inside the thing."

"What does it look like?"

"Bright. Very bright. Lots of machines along the side. The walls are slightly curved. Only the floor seems flat."

"What are the machines?"

"I don't know. I've never seen anything like them. Even in the science fiction movies. One or two have screens and there are lines bouncing across them. There are colored lights. Not the little blinking lights like on our computers, but bigger, strangely shaped lights."

"What made you think they were computers?"

"That's what they look like."

"Where are the aliens?"

"I don't know where they went. There are only two of them left with me. They stand looking at me, but are closer to the machines. One of them is touching the machines."

49

"What do his hands look like?"

"Claws. He has three fingers."

"Why do you say he?" (I realized after playing back the tape that I had used the term first.)

"Because he's a male."

"How do you know?"

"Because the woman were different. Like real women."

That stumped me. "Like real women?"

"They have longer hair. And breasts. I could see that they had breasts. One of them wore a long skirt and had a band around her head."

I sat back in the chair, almost unbelieving. Here were two points from other cases that had been thrown into the story almost casually. In both the Roach abduction and the Llanca abduction (I'm dealing with the cases chronologically and not in order of their reports. In other words, I had already studied the Llanca case when I learned of the Ramstead report.) there was mention made of a female or females. Debbie Roach had talked about the Indian girl. Llanca had described a woman.

The hypnotist pointed to her watch. I looked at the time and saw that nearly an hour had passed. We would have to end the session. We hadn't gotten very far, except to learn that an abduction had taken place. The hypnotist told Susan to relax and forget all that she had told us, to relax for a few minutes.

Across the room, the three of us, John Ramstead, the hypnotist, and I, held a quick conference. The hypnotist had given Susan the suggestion to not remember any of the regression so that we could continue the next day without having Susan worry about it all night. When we finished the investigation, we could remove the block and let her remember it all.

I glanced at John and whispered, "Providing that you want to continue."

50

"Oh, hell yes," he said. "We'll want to see this to the very end."

I cautioned John not to say anything. It would be best if they tried to ignore this for now, although Susan would want to know what had been discussed and what she had said. The less that John said at this juncture, the better. We didn't want to color Susan's statements by saying something to her too early. The best thing would be for him to refuse to answer questions, but to tell her when it was over that we would play the tapes for her, if she wanted to hear them. But by that time she would remember it all anyway. John agreed.

We met the following day in the same place. Susan went into the trance quickly and we were able to pick up where we had left off. I asked about the women again. How they were dressed.

"Almost like the men. One of them wore a long skirt, but the other had worn a jumpsuit like the men."

"Can you describe it?"

"It was metallic, silver or gray. It was all in one piece, even the gloves and boots. There was a belt that went across the chest and fastened to a belt that wrapped around the waist."

"What are these people doing?"

"They're not people. Like people but not really people."

"What are they doing?"

"The male is standing near the table. The woman in the long skirt comes toward me and made a gesture with her hands."

"Did she have real hands?"

"No. Her hands were like the others."

"How did she gesture?"

"She moved one hand up and down in front of her."

"Do you know what that means?"

"I think she wants me to take off my clothes."

"What do you do?"

"I shake my head no and try to back away slightly. She follows me and makes the same gesture. When I refused again, she reached for the top button of my blouse. I pushed her hand away and then the others came toward me."

I checked my notes and found that we had a problem. She had talked about two creatures remaining with her but now was talking about three of them. I didn't like that. I asked, "How many are in the room with you?"

"Now?"

"Yes."

"Five."

"Did you see them enter?"

"No. I was watching the creature with the long skirt. While she was trying to get me to take off my clothes, the others must have come back."

"Go on."

"I didn't take off my clothes, but two of them grabbed my arms. I tried to struggle but felt the will drain out of me. I didn't care what they did. I just wanted it all to end."

"Are you frightened?"

"Not any more. They told me it wouldn't be much longer. The woman says that they have to get the information. That it's very important. I don't care about that. I just want it to end."

"What's happening now?"

"The woman in the long skirt reached up and unbuttoned my blouse and pushed it off my shoulders. Then they let go and I let it fall to the floor. But now I begin to undress. Somehow it just seems easier than to resist them. I strip to my panties but I refused to take them off."

"After you were undressed, what happened?"

"I don't know. I don't remember." She wrinkled her brow, as if concentrating but said nothing more.

"Sure you can," I said. "You made it through it in good shape. Now we need to know about it. You can remember if you try."

"They guided me to the table and made me get up on it. I stretch out on it. That's all I remember."

"Is that all you remember or is it all you want to remember?"

"That's all I remember."

I decided not to push at the point. I could come back to it later. It was a phenomenon that I had seen before. Pat Roach had said she was examined but that she didn't want to talk about it. After a few sessions, as we kept pushing, the blocks crumbled and we could get at the information. Now it was time to fill in the finer details.

"What's happening now?"

"I'm putting on my clothes. It's funny.

"What's funny?"

"I have to put on all my clothes, but I don't remember taking them all off."

This was too good of an opportunity to let pass. I asked, "Did they remove the last of your clothes during the exam?"

"Yes."

53

"What did they do?"

"I don't know. It's hard to remember."

"Why is that?"

"They told me that I wouldn't remember after I woke in the car."

"What wouldn't you remember?"

"Everything. All that I would remember is the strange light. I wouldn't remember anything else."

I remembered Harder's question to Pat Roach. "Have you ever been hypnotized before?"

"Only on the ship."

"The alien ship?"

"Yes."

"What did they do during the exam?"

"I don't remember."

The hypnotist jumped in. "That's all right. You don't have to remember now. You were getting dressed. What happened when you were dressed."

"They didn't help at all. I don't feel good. My stomach hurts and my knees ache, but they don't seem to notice. They have all left again, except for one male and the female in the long skirt. They watch me but don't bother to help. They seem impatient and I get the feeling that they want me to hurry so that they can get me out of there."

There was so much that I wanted to know, but I didn't want to lead her. I wanted her to add information without my giving her any ideas. Phrasing the questions was becoming a problem. I remembered the human that Pat Roach had talked about and wondered if there was a man on the ship with Susan. But how to ask without planting the idea? And what about the line of people that Debbie Roach had talked about? I wanted to know if there were others involved, but I had to wait patiently for her to volunteer the information.

"You're dressed now," I said. "What happened next?"

"The door opens and the two of them help me outside. I move my feet like I'm walking but it feels like I'm floating. We step across the highway and they open my car door and put me inside. They tell me to wait a minute and then I will see the ship in the sky."

"They talked to you?"

"No." She hesitated. "I just knew it, I guess."

"And the ship left?"

"There was a buzzing sound from it. I don't think it spun. The sound got louder and suddenly it was high in the sky."

I nodded to the hypnotist and she said, "All right, Susan. I want you to relax now. In a few minutes you will awaken. I will tell you when you can."

Again we held a quick, quiet conference. I suggested that we now had the story, other than the minor details that we could fill in later. Now might be the time to let her remember what she had told us. She could digest the idea for a couple of hours and then maybe we could get at the details of the examination. The hypnotist agreed.

John said, "Hasn't it occurred to either of you that this has been too easy? You put her under hypnosis and she spills her guts. I would think that aliens who could manipulate the situations as well as they seem to would be able to shut off all memory of such an experience so that it would take more than a couple of sessions and a couple of amateur sleuths to get at."

Although I didn't say anything, I had to agree. The aliens seemed to set it up and then mark it with a flag that said, "Don't hypnotize me." Naturally the first thing we did was hypnotize her. They tried to cover their tracks, but only slightly. That didn't make too much sense.

But then maybe it came back to what Pat Roach had said a couple of years earlier. Maybe they didn't understand us or how our minds work. Many of the things that I was seeing suggested that they were interested in studying our mental processes. Without more information, maybe they didn't understand how to set up stronger blocks. Maybe they did the best they could. Or maybe it was only a few people who had broken through the blocks and told us their stories. It was possible that we were looking at only the tip of the iceberg.

The hypnotist went back to Susan and said, "All right, you will awaken in a moment. You will be able to remember the events we have discussed and some of the things that we didn't. You will think of it as the past and not be greatly bothered by it."

Susan came out of it looking tense. Her face was lined and there was perspiration on her upper lip. She was trembling and her husband held her hand. She didn't speak for several minutes and then said, simply, "Wow." After a few minutes, Susan seemed to be fine, drained but fine. She said that it took a moment to get used to it, but that she was all right, and she was hungry. That seemed to be a good way to unwind. We could have dinner and then possibly fit in another session, if Susan felt up to it.

After dinner, we discussed the case. John Ramstead was amazed that all this had happened, and that neither he nor his wife had ever suspected. He had asked her what she had been doing and she had said watching the UFO. She had explained about her car engine dying and the radio failing, but neither of them had ever thought to check the times because each believed that the other knew exactly how long the sighting had lasted. John would say what took you so long to answer and she would say that the radio was out. Because the discussion would upset Susan, they would never pursue it too far. Without the clue of time discrepancy, there was no reason to suspect that an abduction had taken place.

Susan added more details as the memories of that night came flooding to her. She told us that the boots the aliens wore had toes in them. There was a division between the big toe and the others. She thought, based on their hands, that they had only two or three toes.

There was also a screen at one end of the ship. It seemed that it was showing the outside because she thought she could see stars on it, but then remembered the night had been overcast. The stars were something else. Thoughts of both Betty Hill and Pat Roach came to mind; both had seen what they thought were either stars or star charts.

Finally we came back to the examination. Susan remembered being strapped to the table. Both hands were strapped down, but only one leg. She remembered seeing her blood flow into a series of small tubes as needles were pushed into her arms. She said she watched it with a detached amusement, as if it was happening to someone else.

We kept talking about it. Susan would remember something new about the exam. She had been uncomfortable because her arms had been stretched out so that they were straight. It was as if the aliens had pulled them as far as they could before strapping them to the table. She said that she would notice that she was tense and would relax slightly, only to tense again. She said that there was a strap around one ankle and around the knee of the same leg, but the other leg was free. She felt prickling along the leg that was strapped and along both arms, but part of the time she didn't know what was happening.

I asked a few pointed questions about the exam, but Susan said that she couldn't remember. Then almost as an aside, she talked about a tube pushed into her body. A cold, metal tube that entered her. She blushed as she mentioned it and then went on to other things. She knew nothing of being hypnotized on the ship. She didn't remember them finishing the job of stripping her, but she did remember having to put on all her clothes. She couldn't remember them strapping her down, but did remember things after that happened, and she remembered them unbuckling the straps.

When we had everything that we could get, I suggested that we try one more session. I made it clear that we wanted to know about the exam, and that Susan had been reluctant to talk about it under hypnosis. She said that it didn't worry her now, and that she wanted to know what had been done to her. With that attitude, I thought that we could probably break through the last barrier.

Susan slipped under again easily. The hypnotist suggested that everything was fine. Reminded her that she had gotten out in good shape. "You will remember everything that happened to you, but you won't be frightened."

To start the session, I said, "You were examined."

"Yes."

"How?"

She described being strapped to the table. She said that their hands were cold, almost like the dead and that had frightened her. A band was put around her head so that she could only use her eyes to look around. She watched as the blood samples, as well as some skin scrapings were taken. They forced her mouth open and took more samples. They prodded her abdomen and she saw a needle, long and thin, descend toward her. She couldn't see if it was being held by one of the creatures or by the machine. She felt it penetrate her belly button.

At that point she wanted to scream, may have screamed, but the pain faded, replaced by a feeling of euphoria. She felt her mind begin to drift, as if toward sleep. She turned her eyes to the right and saw a creature standing there, and he seemed to be telling her to sleep. To relax and they would talk.

To the left, she saw that something had been pushed forward so that it touched the table near her left hand. She studied it for a moment and then looked to the screen. She thought that she could see her blood coursing through her veins, her lungs expanding and contracting as she breathed, and she felt her heart hammering in her chest. She watched that until she slipped into a deeper sleep.

The psychological probing was done with even less finesse. The first thing she noticed was that the male questioning her never moved his lips. She knew what he wanted to know and was powerless to stop the memories and emotions from flooding her. One minute she was unusually happy and the next feeling as if her heart would break. The creature guided her through her happiest moments and her worst. She was forced to relive incidents as if they were just happening while the machines near her flashed and buzzed and recorded it all. The kaleidoscope range of feelings left her drained and sick to her stomach.

And there seemed to be no logical progression. The male made her jump from one memory to another, as if he wanted to see how quickly he could mess her up, or how badly he could make her feel. It seemed like an experiment in conditioned response as the aliens learned which buttons caused which reactions.

When she had run the emotional gauntlet through her mind, he introduced outside terrors. She was panicked, calmed, terrified, and then left for a moment, believing that they were going to take her to their home world as an exhibit. She would be left where other members of the alien race could make her relive her emotions so they could feel them too.

Finally the mental tests ended and another machine was brought closer to her. It was centered between her legs and she felt the cold metal of the device enter her slowly. She screamed then and the sensation vanished. She felt herself filled and then the metal tube was withdrawn.

Throughout the session, the hypnotist had to keep interrupting to remind Susan that it was all in the past and there was nothing that the creatures could do to her now. They had returned her to her car, just as they had said they would. They had calmed her, and made her forget. She was safe now.

When the aliens finished with her, one of them unbuckled one of the straps around her wrists and the one around her head. They let her finish the job. There were red marks about both wrists, her knee and ankle, where the straps had been that faded quickly. Both hands and her leg tingled as if they had gone to sleep. The creatures did nothing to relieve the pain there, or to stop her from getting dressed. They didn't help either.

Once again she described getting dressed. I said, "The hypnotic blocks they use are not very effective."

"Because they don't really care. They know that we can get through them if we can find the right people, but they don't care if we do or not. They use the blocks to gain time and keep some of the information from people."

I sat back and looked at her. There were a dozen questions that raced through my head. Things that I wanted to ask, but the hypnotist was talking to Susan, trying to wipe away her agitation while I tried to organize my thoughts. Her answer to the question had made no sense. No reason to advertise, and yet no reason to hide it too deeply because there wasn't a lot that we could do about it. If I hadn't asked the right question in the right circumstances, we might never have known about this case. How many others were there that we didn't know about? How could we ever find them? It was only by the sheerest of coincidence that Susan and her husband had been in CB contact, and that he noticed twenty minutes passing while she thought it was five.

The same could be said about the Roach abduction. The aliens had worked to keep her from knowing about the abduction, but let the youngest daughter remember everything. It didn't seem likely that the aliens would realize that we paid very little attention to young children who told strange stories. Still, Pat remembered something as did Bonnie. The sense of it all vanished in a whirlpool of confusion that I was powerless to unscramble.

To Susan I said, "How do you know that they don't care?"

"The one who asked the questions told me. I said that they were hurting me and he said that he didn't care. The data was important. Only the data."

I was about to ask another question when Susan spoke again. She said, "There's more but I don't know what it is and you won't be able to get it. Not until conditions are right. Can I wake up now?"

I looked at the hypnotist and she was smiling. She whispered to me. "Asking to wake up isn't that strange." Again, Susan was brought out of it so that she would remember but not be troubled by the ordeal. She would have the same detachment about the incident as if she had remembered it from the day it had happened. It wouldn't frighten her anymore.

Fully awake, she again added details. This time she told us that the creatures had unlocked her car and lifted her out. A truck was parked on the opposite side of the road, a couple of hundred feet in front of her, but she couldn't see the license number. There was no one near the truck.

I felt shivers run down my spine. Confirmation. And yet it wasn't because there was no way to find out who was driving the truck. I asked if she thought she might remember the numbers under hypnosis and she said that she remembered thinking she wished she could see the numbers but couldn't. I filed the information for later use. I had already realized that this wouldn't be the last session. There were too many things that needed to be discussed. (Under hypnosis she still couldn't see the truck's numbers. She did remember that it was gone when she was taken out of the ship.)

When we finished talking about it, Susan and her husband left. I stayed behind to talk to the hypnotist. I wanted to hear her impressions of the case. Someone who hadn't been directly involved in the incident or in UFO research.

She said, "I don't know. I believe her. I can't not believe her. Emotions are hard to fake. Embellishing accounts isn't weird. The subject often tries to please the hypnotist so that they elaborate. They say what they think the hypnotist wants to hear. That's why you have to be careful of what you ask and how you ask it. While a subject can't originate material under hypnosis, he can draw on all his experiences and that includes books, movies, and television. That's an awful lot of material."

"But you believe her?" I asked.

"Of course. I believe that she is telling the truth as she believes it."

I knew exactly what she meant. It was the same problem that surrounded the lie detector tests. It only told you if the witness believed, not if the incident had happened. To give Susan Ramstead a lie detector test would only prove that she believed that she had been abducted and somehow that seemed pointless.

61

LEIGH PROCTOR

Like Hickson and Parker, Leigh Proctor remembered her experience without the help of a psychologist or a hypnotist. Like Susan Ramstead, she was subjected to a cruel physical and mental examination on board a spaceship. And like Dionisio Llanca, she was taken from her car by several creatures. Her case became one more proof that something strange happened in October 1973.

Before the incident, Leigh Proctor was a normal, active college sophomore. She was doing well in her classes, had dozens of friends, and no real problems. But, after she walked into the sheriff's office on October 24, 1973, all that changed. It was the one incident that underscored the real possibility that the aliens don't care what happens to the people they abduct, that they are the cold, unfeeling creatures described by Pat Roach.

Where Pat Roach and Susan Ramstead took their experiences in stride, possibly because of the hypnotic block that had been erected on their memories, Leigh Proctor was almost totally ruined by it. Hickson and Parker manifested a number of bizarre side effects, including Parker's almost irrational fear of the aliens, but Proctor took it a step further. Hickson and Parker remained in society, functioning like nothing out of the ordinary had happened. Proctor seemed to drop out. It was her defense against an experience that was too terrifying to remember, but so terrifying she couldn't forget.

Leigh Proctor left college on October 20, 1973, to spend a day or two at home. She had gotten a late start and later said that she was thinking about skipping her Monday classes to extend her visit. Her parents knew she was coming and when she didn't arrive, they called the sheriff.

William H. Schaller wasn't very concerned about it when the call came in. Proctor was only a couple of hours late, and although it was after midnight, he expected that Proctor would reach home safely. As routine procedure, he alerted his deputies so that they could be on the lookout for the girl, but never actually initiated a search.

About four the following morning, one of the deputies found an abandoned MGB sitting by the side of the road with its hood up, lights on, and the engine running. On the seat the deputy found Proctor's purse which contained all her identification and her money. Near the front of the car, he found one of her shoes and an area that suggested some kind of struggle had taken place.

An extensive police search turned up little other evidence. Schaller said, "In one of the nearby fields, we found several sets of footprints and a heavier track indicating that something had been dragged. But the tracks ended abruptly and we found no other evidence." Schaller found those details interesting but couldn't assign any real value to the find because he didn't have enough information to work with.

Fearing the worst, they spent three days combing the surrounding countryside, hoping to find some trace of the missing girl. Scuba divers checked farm ponds and a rock quarry; dragging operations were discussed but never initiated. The sheriff was baffled and didn't have much hope. Not after her abandoned car and purse were found.

But the field investigations ended abruptly when Proctor walked into the sheriff's office and almost calmly asked to use the phone. Schaller knew who she was because he had looked at the picture of her that was taped to a bulletin board nearly every hour as the search progressed. He asked a few questions which she refused to answer until she could use the phone. When Schaller saw how badly her hands were shaking he gave her the phone to call home and decided to wait for her parents before trying to question her.

During the twenty minutes it took Proctor's parents to arrive, the sheriff offered the young woman a cup of coffee which she refused. She sat in a chair in the corner, her eyes on the floor. Schaller was concerned because she looked like she might be going into emotional shock. Schaller later told investigators that he looked her over carefully to make sure that she wasn't hurt. He was afraid that she had been in an accident of some kind, although her car hadn't been damaged. Her feet were dirty and her pantyhose badly ripped. Her skirt was torn along one seam. Schaller asked her several times if she wanted a doctor or something to eat, but she just shook her head.

After her parents arrived and talked to her for nearly fifteen minutes, she seemed to be able to calm down enough to explain where she had been.

The following narration was put together based on the participants memories and the tape recorded statement made by Leigh Proctor.

Slowly, haltingly, she began to tell the story. She was driving along the deserted highway about 10:00 p.m. when the lights dimmed, the engine sputtered and died, and the car rolled to a halt. Leigh got out and opened the hood, hoping that she would find something wrong that she could fix easily. She didn't hear anyone approach but was suddenly grabbed from behind. Startled, she screamed and resisted, but stopped abruptly when one of the "creatures" stepped in front of her.

It was obvious that Leigh was becoming agitated by the memories and the questioning was momentarily stopped. When she regained her control, the sheriff asked her to describe the creatures.

"There were three of them. They seemed to have no real face. Only white faces like a molded plastic mask. They had two large eyes set close to the side of the head. And the hands. Not real hands like ours. More like a claw with three fingers."

The sheriff asked, "Can you remember what they were wearing?" He later admitted that he hadn't believed her story but felt that he should question her so that he could learn what had actually happened.

"Some sort of a metallic blue coverall, with a white stripe down the side."

"What happened after you realized that they weren't people?"

Leigh described how she was floated to a domed disc that was sitting in a nearby field. She was forced into a room where she was stripped, strapped to a table and given a complete physical examination that included blood tests, skin scrapings and a rectal exam. Several needles had been pushed into her arms and abdomen. The exam seemed to last for hours, but Leigh couldn't be sure.

Schaller asked to see the needle marks on her arms. When Leigh pushed up the sleeve of her blouse, he was mildly surprised to see what appeared to be needle marks, which reinforced his opinion that the story was some kind of drug induced hallucination. But when she unbuttoned her blouse and showed him the needle marks on her stomach, Schaller was puzzled and asked to see the backs of her knees, which were unmarked. Schaller later explained that had Leigh been an addict, he would have expected needle marks on the backs of her knees, but not on her stomach.

Leigh said that she was then left alone in the brightly lighted exam room for a long time, perhaps several hours, still strapped to the table. Eventually she was released and strapped to a chair. Electrodes resembling those of a polygraph machine were attached to her body and she was interrogated at length by two creatures. After some time, the interrogators left the room, leaving Leigh strapped to the chair, hands fastened behind it, and hooked to the machine.

Some time later, one of them returned and released her, gave her something that appeared to be food and water, although she was afraid to eat it. She drank the water which tasted just like water. She was left alone again. She was unsure how much time passed because she fell asleep.

At this point Schaller interrupted her to say that he was surprised that she could sleep under the circumstances.

66

"I don't know," she replied. "Maybe they put something into the water. All I know is that I was suddenly very tired."

When she awakened, they returned with her clothes, including the one shoe, the other having been lost in the struggle at the car. They watched her dress, and then questioned her, but did not restrain her.

Once again she was left along for a long time. Leigh said that she thought that they might be watching her during the periods of isolation. When they returned, they brought more food and water. This time hunger had won out and she ate some of the food too. She said that it was tasteless, like chewing a wad of paper. After eating, she again fell asleep.

She awoke alone, but noticed that they had been back again. They had taken her watch, earrings, and the one shoe. She sat up amazed to notice she was no longer in the ship but in a cornfield.

"I got to my feet and followed the rows, which took me to a road, and I started walking. After a while I realized that I was on the road to town. The only thing I could think of was to get to the sheriffs office and call home."

Since by now it was after one in the morning, the consensus of opinion was that the best thing to do was let Leigh go home with her parents and get some rest. Before the Proctor's left, however, Schaller pulled Leigh's father aside and told him that there were a lot of unanswered questions. He wanted to talk to Leigh again and suggested that he could drive out to the farm that afternoon.

That afternoon, Schaller and a man experienced in hypnotic regression techniques, Dr. James A. Richardson, drove to the Proctor farm. Leigh told the story again, adding very little to it. Schaller then suggested that they try hypnosis because it could get at the details that Leigh might have forgotten, and Richardson could make a post hypnotic suggestion that would make the experience a little less real and a little less painful.

Leigh was reluctant at first. Richardson said that he could put her into a light trance to let her see what hypnosis was like, and then later, if she wanted, they could explore the abduction. Leigh agreed to try it.

After the experimental session, Leigh agreed to hypnosis, if her parents were allowed to stay in the room. Richardson put her into another light trance and regressed her to the night of the incident. He told her that she was standing on the highway and that her car was stalled. The hood was up and she was looking at the engine. He asked, "What do you remember."

"I'm grabbed from behind. My first thought is that some of my friends must be playing a trick on me. That is, I think that when one of them steps around in front of me, and I see that he's wearing a Halloween mask. Then I realize that it couldn't be any of my friends and suddenly I'm very frightened. I wonder if someone is going to rape me, then I realize that there's more than one of them and they all look alike. I know they aren't human."

"How do you know that?"

Because they all stand about five feet tall and are wearing shiny blue coveralls. They have belts that go from the shoulder to the waist and there seems to be a carrying case of some kind attached to the belt. I have the impression that they are wearing gloves and boots, but no helmet. I think that is strange because they always wear helmets on TV. Their faces are void of features and I wonder if they might be wearing masks of some kind so that they can breathe our air. When one of them steps close to me and touches something to the side of my neck, I seem to lose the will to resist and let them drag me away."

"Go on."

"Two of them are pulling me along by the arms and the third one is walking ahead of us. We are in a field, not far from my car, and I can see it sitting there on five metal fins."

"What's sitting there? Your car?" "It looks sort of like a Frisbee with a very short, flat topped cylinder on top and a little dome on top of that. I am thinking that I always thought it would be interesting to see a flying saucer, but this is a lot closer than I ever wanted to get to one. I can see that there is an opening in the side with a ramp sloping down, and I realize they are going to take me inside of it and I want to run away, but I can't."

For the next hour or so, Richardson and Schaller questioned Leigh about her story. She remembered more details of the examinations but did not alter the story significantly. She went into more detail, was more precise in her answers. When it ended, Schaller could feel the sweat standing on his forehead and soaking through his shirt. Leigh's parents were nearly in a state of shock.

Richardson finally told Leigh to relax and to sleep. He was going to count to ten and as he spoke each number she was going to become a little more awake. And she would forget as much of the incident as she wanted to, but would be able to recall it again, under hypnosis.

Leigh woke up extremely agitated because she remembered almost the entire ordeal. The images were so vividly impressed in her mind that Richardson's suggestion to forget had no effect.

On the way back to town, Schaller asked Richardson what he had thought of the case. Richardson said that his first impression was that Leigh had had a vivid dream or hallucination, but the deeper he probed, the more he was convinced that something real had happened to the girl. He pointed out that the needle marks were real. And she had been missing for four days, and she had to be somewhere. Richardson thought that Schaller should try to find that somewhere, because that would certainly answer some of the questions.

During the next two months, Schaller tried to find an explanation that fit all the facts. A drug induced hallucination was eventually ruled out because neither Leigh's parents nor her friends remembered her ever using drugs. Occasionally she would drink, but rarely. And she had no police record, either in her hometown or at college.

Although he looked, he couldn't find anyone who remembered seeing or even who claimed to have seen Leigh during the four days that she was missing. She apparently hadn't used a motel room, bought food, or slept in the bus station. No one remembered her. No taxi drivers or bus drivers had seen her. And of course, she hadn't bought any gas because the sheriff had her car impounded after they found it on the highway.

Schaller and Richardson convinced Leigh that she should take a lie detector test. If the case was an outright lie, then something should turn up on the machine. But, when it was over, the operator concluded that she had told no lies. He pointed out that it didn't mean she had been abducted by a flying saucer crew, only that she believed that she had been. The operator wanted to make the distinction clear.

Schaller even convinced Leigh and her parents that she should see a psychiatrist because she was so upset about the incident. He might be able to help her conquer some of her anxiety. Leigh didn't believe that it would help, but went along because everyone seemed to be insisting.

And when the psychiatrist concluded that there were no psychic reasons for her story, that she was as stable as could be expected, considering what she believed, Schaller was about ready to accept the story. In desperation he contacted a local UFO investigator to find out if there had been any other UFO reports that night, or on the nights that Leigh was missing.

To his surprise he learned that the country was in the middle of a flap, a period of intense UFO activity. Schaller decided to narrow the limits of his question and ask only about the area where Leigh had been found.

There were a couple of sightings. The first one seemed to be Venus. The second was of a domed disc that was seen at low altitude, but Schaller couldn't find the witness. He had given a false name and fake phone number. The UFO investigator said that it was common. Someone had thought that the information should get to someone who could use it, but who didn't want to be harassed by seven thousand self proclaimed UFO investigators. Without the source of the information, the case was virtually useless, except that it seemed to confirm that a UFO had been in the area.

In most abductions, the story ends with the investigators stumped, but willing to believe the witness. The witness has provided clues and told long tales under hypnosis. After the excitement dies down, the witness returns to a fairly normal life. Hickson and Parker's case differed slightly because they got national attention.

They had the opportunity to tell the world their story. For several weeks, they received hundreds of letters and phone calls. But even all that attention didn't destroy their lives.

Leigh wasn't that lucky. Schaller learned the rest of the story when he decided to make a follow up investigation. He thought that a couple of months away from the case would give him the distance to see something that he hadn't seen before. Without calling, he drove out to the Proctor farm.

Leigh's parents appeared uncomfortable when Schaller arrived. They hesitated before telling him that Leigh had dropped out of college. She had been afraid to return. She had become progressively more withdrawn. The Proctors had tried to help their daughter deal with the experience, but their attempts only seemed to reinforce the memories and Leigh moved out of the house.

Schaller pushed, trying to find out more. Leigh's father finally agreed to try to phone her, but she didn't answer. He explained that she often didn't answer the phone but that she was probably there because she never went anywhere. He told Schaller that he and his wife had to take her food because Leigh would forget to buy groceries. With some reluctance, he provided Schaller with the address.

Later Schaller would say, "I couldn't believe the building. It was slowly decaying. It probably had once been a hotel but that was long before my time. The carpeting in the hallway was threadbare and stained. The paint was beginning to peel and blister. The environment seemed to underscore the whole incident.

"The inside of her apartment was even worse," Schaller continued. "The room was littered with papers and clothes and rotting food. There was an open cereal box and three different open packs of cigarettes on the coffee table near a dirty old couch. The room was stifling and dark. The shades

71

were drawn and there was an old blanket tacked to the wall partially covering one window."

Schaller said that there were dishes stacked in the sink and there was the unmistakable odor of garbage that had stayed too long, made even more potent by the heat in the apartment.

Before she had opened the door, Leigh had told Schaller that she wasn't dressed yet and for him to wait a moment before coming in. Now she came out of the bedroom, wearing a long tailed flannel shirt that came about halfway to her knees and little else. Her hair looked as if it hadn't been combed in a week or washed in two. There was a smudge of some kind on her nose, and dark circles under her eyes. Her face was very thin. Schaller said later that he was shocked by her appearance. She had lost fifteen or twenty pounds and she had not been heavy to begin with. Schaller later confided to investigators that this was the first time that he suspected that the alien kidnapping was something more than a hallucination.

When Schaller asked her what had happened, Leigh told him, in no uncertain terms. She said that she couldn't sleep at night because she would be thinking about them. She couldn't sleep during the day for the same reasons. Her family tried to help but they would only get in the way. They had made things worse, so she had moved out.

After a few minutes Schaller decided that Leigh didn't need him asking anymore questions and he excused himself. Several hours later he returned, because he remembered seeing a box of .38 bullets sitting on one of the tables. He was suddenly afraid that she was going to use the .38 on herself.

It was early morning when he returned. After banging on the door for several minutes, Leigh opened it. She was still wearing the flannel shirt and she appeared to have been drinking continuously since Schaller had left.

Schaller asked about the revolver and could think of no delicate way of asking if she planned on killing herself, so he blurted out the question.

It was then that she filled in the final details of the abduction. The details that hadn't come out under hypnosis, but details that had plagued her for weeks afterward. They had told her they would be back. They would look for her, to see how she was doing, to see how she was fitting in. And they would return because they were sure that she would want to see the baby.

She told Schaller that the pistol wasn't for her suicide, but for the aliens, if they came back. She didn't want to see them, or any baby they might have, regardless of where it had come from. Schaller called the UFO expert to find out if the creatures ever did return to any of the scenes.

He said that the records show that the aliens often tell the victims that they are coming back, but they never do. Schaller called Leigh and told her that, but it didn't help then. Later, as she forced herself out of her depression, the one hope she could cling to was that they never came back even though they told other victims that they would.

In the end, Schaller, Richardson, and the others, believed Leigh Proctor. Schaller summed it up the best when he said, "I don't care what anyone says about flying saucers or UFO's or whatever. I believe that Leigh is telling the truth, and I believe the truth to be that she was abducted by aliens from space."

DIONISIO LLANCA

On October 31, Dionisio Llanca woke up in the hospital and finally remembered seeing the UFO. He had been there for three days with total amnesia and it was on Wednesday that he remembered. He remembered the flying saucer, remembered the creatures and he began to remember what they had done to him.

Late on Saturday evening, October 27, Llanca woke from his nap and ate dinner. He relaxed for a few minutes and then prepared to leave on an all night driving job. About 12:30 a.m. on Sunday morning, he climbed into the cab of his truck and told his uncle, "Good-bye." About thirty minutes later he stopped for gas, looked at the tires and saw that the left rear was low. He decided that it would be all right and drove out of Bahia Blanca, Argentina. A few miles out of town, the tire went flat and he had to change it alone and in the dark.

He pulled to the shoulder of the road, climbed out of the truck and set up the jack. As he worked, he noticed that there were lights in the distance, like those of an approaching car. He thought nothing of them until they increased in intensity and came closer. When the light changed to a brilliant blue, like that of an arc welder's torch, Llanca became interested. He tried to stand but couldn't. The whole area was bright with the strange blue light.

Llanca struggled to get up, to look to the woods near the road but his muscles wouldn't respond, his body being paralyzed. Then, hovering just off the ground, near his truck, he saw a dome topped disc and standing near him, under the UFO were the creatures from it. Again he tried to stand and again he failed. He tried to scream at them, to make them go away, but he couldn't speak. The paralysis was spreading by then, making his body weak while the creatures just stood near him, studying him.

There were three of them, two males and one was obviously female. They were humanoid with long blond hair and elongated eyes. They were wearing one piece silver flying suits, high boots, gloves that extended up their arms, but no belts or weapons or helmets. Llanca felt like a trapped animal, only he couldn't run or hide or move. He could only watch the creatures. They talked among themselves for several seconds, in voices that sounded like a badly tuned radio full of chirps, buzzes and static. Finally one of the men reached out, grabbed Llanca by the neck of his sweater and firmly lifted him. Panic spread; he wanted to run or fight but couldn't do either. He tried to scream but there was no sound.

One of the creatures held him and another put a small black box against his left index finger. Peace began drifting through him and he relaxed though still afraid. The box was held against his finger for several seconds and when it was removed, there were drops of blood on his hand. Then, he must have fainted because he remembered nothing else.

Early in the morning, Llanca awoke, cold and wet. He was lying in deep grass and didn't know who he was, where he was, or how he had gotten there. When he sat up he could see cars moving in the distance. For minutes he sat, staring toward the road, and then, slowly, he got up and walked to it. He stumbled along, feeling sick, cold and alone.

As the sun came up and the ground fog dissipated, a man stopped to give Llanca a ride. Emmanuel Ortega could see that Llanca wasn't well and at seven in the morning, checked him into the Bahia Blanca hospital. Doctor Richardo Smiroff was on duty and began the examination. There were no signs of physical injuries but when the doctor tried to touch him, Llanca drew away, afraid.

For three days they worked, trying to restore Llanca's memory. Little by little, they brought the memories to the surface. On Wednesday morning

Llanca suddenly remembered almost everything. He had seen a flying saucer close to the ground and he had seen the crew. But, he couldn't remember the first few hours of Sunday morning. It was a complete blank and it was that period that the doctors wanted to reveal.

Using hypnotic regression techniques they began to trace the lost hours. Llanca subconsciously fought them. He would talk of the creatures with the elongated eyes picking him up, using their strange little box and then that the creatures spoke to him.

Over the next few days, the doctors put the story together. Llanca again and again talked about the strange blue light, the three beings and the trip to the hospital but the early morning hours remained a mystery. Doctor Eladio Santos, a hypnotist and Doctor Eduardo Mata, a psychologist, asked him to submit to the use of Pentothal. Under its influence Llanca told more about the spaceship, the creatures and the missing hours. The tapes of the Llanca interviews covered the same ground over and over. To get him to talk the doctors found that they had to cover each step a dozen times. To help the flow of the report, many of the repetitions have been eliminated.

Llanca was falling under the influence of the drug and the doctors waited a few minutes before they tried to take him back to when he first noticed the lights. He said that he was paralyzed and couldn't move. Then he saw the creatures...

"No! No! Please! Don't do anything to me! Who are you? What do you want...take the truck and the silver but don't do anything to me."

Llanca looked like he wanted to move, wanted to run, but couldn't. The paralysis was obvious to the doctors and they tried to lead the questioning away from it.

"Who are you seeing?" one of them asked.

"Them. Two men...and also a woman."

"How are they dressed?

"They have on silvery suits, very tight fitting, and boots...and gloves."

"What color are the gloves?"

77

Slowly, quietly, as if fighting through pain, he said, "Yellow. Yellow-orange."

"Do they speak to you?"

"No... I sense a buzzing noise. Like a beehive."

"Do they threaten you?"

"No..." Llanca's eyes widened in fright. "One comes near me. He took my hand...pricked me with a device."

"Did that hurt?"

"No..." Llanca seemed to relax then, as if the terror he was experiencing because of the strangers and their machine had left him. He was still sweating, but no longer frightened.

"What does the device look like?"

"An electric shaver..."

"What are they doing now?"

"They carry me. Where are they taking me?" Again it looked as if Llanca wanted to fight them but there was something holding him back. "I go up with the men," he said.

"Where are you going up to? Did you use stairs?"

"No...on a ray of light." The answers were slow in coming as if Llanca had to fight to answer each question.

"What are you seeing now?"

"The floor is like lead...silvery...gray...there is only one window...it's round."

"Go on."

"There are many devices, many of them, two viewing screens. In one, stars can be seen..."

By now Llanca had been under the influence of the drug for over two hours and the strain was apparent. The memories were just not surfacing as they should have.

He had to fight to bring each one to the surface and it seemed that he had been given a strong post-hypnotic command not to remember anything about the incident. The aliens from the flying saucer didn't want Llanca talking about the craft or what had happened on it and had tried to wipe it from his conscious mind. They had gotten overly ambitious and had taken all his conscious memories for the missing three days.

The doctors found the story itself hard to believe. The emotions exhibited by Llanca seemed quite real, but that didn't mean that Llanca had actually been aboard an alien spacecraft. They began to search for a more conventional answer and for more evidence. Llanca told them about his truck then, the silver hidden it in and where he had been when the tire had gone flat. When they went to check, the truck was still by the side of the road with one of the tires off. In the cab was just over five thousand pesos in silver coin. They didn't believe that Llanca would leave that kind of money lying around, even to prove his story. All the outside facts seemed to support Llanca's claim.

The next session was even more trying, more unbelievable, more impossible. Llanca responded to the drug faster and as Doctor Mata started his tape recorder, he asked, "Do the crew speak to you?"

"The radio speaks to me."

"What language does it speak?"

"Spanish."

"Do they tell you where they are from?"

"They say that is their secret..."

"Have they spoken to other people from Earth?"

Suddenly Llanca froze. He didn't move for several seconds and then said, almost inaudibly said, "Yes, since 1960."

79

"What are they doing?"

Again there was a long delay before Llanca could force out an answer. "They wish to learn if we can live in their world?"

"Why?"

Llanca sat still, unmoving. He struggled to give an answer but nothing came. The inner turmoil grew as Llanca became more frightened, but he didn't speak.

Hoping for an answer later, they moved on. "What is the place like where you are now?"

"Illuminated... Yellow... It is like a strong box.."

Llanca began to tremble. Talking of the creatures and where they were from only bothered him briefly but now he was reminded of the spaceship. He became frightened, looking from side to side wildly as if he was being held down. He struggled. His emotions, his fright, grew, becoming strong and real. The session had to be ended.

The doctors left Llanca asleep so that they could discuss what they had just heard. People can lie under the influence of drugs and hypnosis, but the lies are easy to spot. Llanca's reactions to his questioning, his emotions were too real to have been faked. He was re-living the experience and he didn't like it. They had to probe carefully or they could cause a permanent psychological injury.

The next day, Llanca was put under again. Doctor Mata began the session at the point it had ended the day before. He told Llanca that he was inside the craft, that it was brightly lighted, yellow and that he had just arrived. "What are you doing now?" he asked.

"My lighter. They have it. It is on the table with my watch and pack of cigarettes." Llanca moved like he was looking around and mumbled a few words before saying, "The woman is wearing black gloves, with small nails in the palm. She is coming nearer. She is going to..."

Llanca tried to move away. He raised his hand to block a blow and closed

80

his eyes to protect them. Suddenly he fell into a very deep sleep. He didn't move for minutes, half an hour. Nothing the doctors did would bring him out of the sleep or make him answer their questions. They yelled at him, told him that time had passed, that he was outside the ship, but he failed to respond. As Llanca continued to sleep, the doctors were becoming frantic. The depth of the trance was beyond anything they had ever seen and nothing would break through it.

Llanca continued to sleep and then as suddenly as he stopped, he began to talk again. "I am falling, falling slowly into a pasture. They have told me that they will search for me later...I am cold...I go to the road and begin to walk about it...Who am I?...Who am I?"

For a few minutes more, the doctors continued to gently probe, staying away from the incident with the female alien and the black glove. They asked Llanca to describe the outside of the UFO and he told them that a cable ran from the ship to a nearby power line and another cable was lowered to a small lake. He didn't know the purpose of either cable.

Just before the session ended, Llanca dropped his bomb. The doctors gently probed, trying to get at the thirty minutes of deep sleep. Llanca suddenly began to talk as if he had a recorded message, not answering questions, just giving information.

"I have a message from the beings in the craft but I can't tell you what it is. No matter what you or any other Earth scientists do, there will remain a memory lapse while I was on the ship. I was there for forty to forty-five minutes."

The session ended. Both doctors wanted to try to find the answers to their questions, but they didn't want to injure Llanca. They felt that they had been challenged by the creatures in the UFO but the block the aliens had erected was too strong for them to break. To press farther could possibly damage Llanca's health or wreck his mind. With nothing more they could do and with Llanca's health restored, they had no choice but to release him.

Doctor Mata wrote a full report about the incident and copies of it were finally forwarded to APRO and eventually sent to me. In the conclusion of his report, Mata said, "We are not eliminating any means of proving that Llanca was not inside a UFO, likewise we are not eliminating any means of proving that he was in one...That which is certain, concrete, is that, under means that in psychiatry are normally useful, such as hypnosis, it has been shown that he was inside a flying saucer and what is more: HE DESCRIBES IT. Added to this is what he describes in his lucid moments. Truthful incidents such as when he describes his entrance into the hospital, those who attend him and an inquisitive nun, etc. Referring to each moment, in the various hypnotic sessions, it is always the same, unchanging."

Doctor Santos explained that it is believed there are three levels or stages in hypnosis. In the third stage, called somnambulistic, the patient is in a very deep trance and will not recall anything about the session unless he is told to. It would seem that the creatures on the UFO may have found a deeper stage, one that we know nothing about. They have discovered how to manipulate it. Maybe they learned the technique from studying Barney and Betty Hill, or Pat Roach or Susan Ramstead. The aliens in each of those reports used hypnotic techniques to force memories from each of the victim's minds. Apparently the UFO scientists have refined the techniques and now are able to completely control the human mind.

Because of all this, the doctors believed that Llanca was telling the truth and is describing the incident as it happened. All the methods used by them, normally successful psychological methods, suggest that the story is true.

The story seemed to be solid and APRO's Coral Lorenzen asked one of the leading weekly newspapers in the United States to find out more if they could. Two reporters were sent to investigate, to interview the doctors, Llanca, and anyone else connected to the case. According to Lorenzen the reporters spent a week alienating the doctors, irritating Llanca and then decided that the case was a hoax designed to promote a new UFO book.

The results of that investigation were published in the APRO BULLETIN but Lorenzen didn't like them. She felt that case was too good to be dropped without confirmation of either the reporter's conclusions or Llanca's story. She contacted APRO Field Investigator Liria D. Jauregui, in Bahia Blanca, and asked that the case be reviewed.

For several weeks Miss Jauregui interviewed the doctors and Llanca. During the sessions she learned many small details that others had overlooked or ignored. She discovered that the UFO crew had examined everything that Llanca had with him that night and then returned it, with one exception. They kept his lighter. Villas-Boas, (see Part IV Appendices: The Alternative

82

View) sixteen years before, said that the aliens from a flying saucer examined all his things and returned them all. Except his lighter. Parallels with other cases began to develop.

The doctors were reluctant to talk because of their concern for their patient. They did tell Jauregui that Llanca was suffering from amnesia within amnesia or in other words, there were things that they couldn't get at, without harming Llanca. They gave her a copy of the tapes of the sessions to help with the investigations. She finally decided that Llanca was telling the truth, there was no book to be publicized and there was little possibility of a hoax.

Like many of the abduction cases, the investigations of the Llanca affair have not been completed and may never be. There is still the missing time and the challenge from the UFO crews. The methods used by the doctors were not able to break through to it. All that can be done had been done and now we wait for the aliens in the flying saucers to give us some of the answers. It seems to be a game to them, but it's certainly no game to those taken on board

THE PATTERN

Even a cursory glance at the data for October 1973 shows that it was different. Where we would expect one abduction report a year on the average, we had five reported and suspected others. In 1947, the wave of sightings consisted mainly of high flying discs and a couple of interesting hoaxes. In 1973 there were at least sixty reports of occupants and a like number of landings. In the occupant reports prior to 1973, we were treated to a variety of aliens ranging from giant creatures with red faces and glowing eyes to short, bean-bag monsters, but in October 1973, we were told of humanoids who were about five feet tall and had big eyes. The wide range of descriptions seemed to seep out of the October 1973 wave. They were replaced with the consistency that the UFO investigators and the scientific community had been demanding. There were some variations, but those could be explained by the fact there were various witnesses.

The few big discrepancies that did appear seemed to underscore the difference in 1973. Hickson and Parker reported gray, robot-like creatures. A few days before that, there had been a report of a similar looking creature. That report had not received the publicity until after Hickson and Parker made their report.

But, we are talking about similarities. Why should Hickson and Parker report wrinkled gray robots while the others claimed to have seen small humanoids that had pasty white faces? Possibly because of the adverse reaction of Hickson and Parker to the gray robot, and because of the underlying causes of the wave.

An examination of the statements of both Hickson and Parker suggest that they were frightened by the strange robots that took them into the alien ship. Parker was so frightened that he passed out. Hickson wasn't in much better shape mentally. It could be that the aliens, realizing that the reaction of both Hickson and Parker were the result of robots, changed their tactics.

Had Hickson and Parker been approached by what they could identify as living beings, they might not have reacted so strongly. In fact, the later abductions show that. True, each of them was frightened by the aliens, but none of them passed out.

Now that makes some sense, especially if the reason for the abduction was to secure information. Not much was learned from Parker. They could measure him, check his respiration, heart beat, blood pressure and the like. The only problem, other than the height and weight was that all the measurements were colored by Parker's reaction to the robots. Had he not passed out, they could have questioned him, but unconscious, he wasn't of much use. They could have gotten the same information by studying television pictures. It may be that after the Hickson-Parker abduction the aliens decided that they needed face to face contact to make sure that the visit wasn't wasted.

From that point on, the descriptions of the creatures fall into a pattern. Humanoid, white faces, elongated eyes, hands that resembled claws, one piece flying suits and gloves and boots. Llanca reported long blond hair on a female creature, but that can be accounted for in the same way that a male's hair might escape notice if he is wearing a hat or a helmet, while the female's hair will usually be longer, at least by some Earth standards. This is another of the facts that suggests a common experience and not another series of hoaxes.

That is to say, if Llanca was making up the information about the sighting, he probably would have followed the information at hand right down the line. He wouldn't have added details that would remove it from the overall pattern, and yet, he describes a long haired female. (We know it was a female because in addition to the long hair, he claimed that she had large breasts while the two males had neither long hair nor large breasts.)

But a female among the aliens isn't all that uncommon. Debbie Roach described an Indian girl. She knew it was an Indian girl because she wore a headband and had on a long dress. Susan Ramstead described much the same thing. It was almost as if they had compared notes before they released their stories, which of course, they hadn't.

Other corroborating details appeared in the reports. Both Leigh Proctor and Susan Ramstead described being strapped down for the examination, but neither knew of the other's story before they were interviewed because neither story had been published prior to the interviews. In fact, both stories appear here for the first time.

86

Further, nearly all the women described the needle that was inserted into the navel. In fact Betty Hill, who reported that she had been abducted in 1961, talked about the needle and suggested that there might be hundreds of little Betty Hills running around space now.

And, many of the witnesses described being hypnotized while on board the alien ship. Pat Roach claimed that they took her thoughts. That they made her relive her childhood experiences. So did Leigh Proctor. It is apparent from Llanca's statements that he, too, was hypnotized by the aliens.

It seems pointless to continue searching for similarities. They abound in the abduction cases. Each witness tells a story that is frighteningly similar. In a few cases they could have read, or heard about the others, but there are at least two where that couldn't have happened. It adds another piece to the puzzle.

Rather than letting the puzzle die there, it seems useful to pursue it a bit farther. Many of the witnesses who reported seeing only occupants, but not abductions, described the creatures and their clothing in a similar fashion. Paul Brown saw two small creatures in silver suits. In Tennessee, a creature with claw like hands reached out to grab two children. In Ohio there was the series of sightings of creatures wearing silver suits. The confirmation from one report to the next continues throughout the wave. One report building on the next but each able to stand alone. One isn't destroyed when it is removed from the pile.

Starting with the beginning of October, we find literally hundreds of reports that seem to be saying the same thing. Small humanoid creatures that ride in relatively small, disc shaped craft carried out an extensive, well coordinated reconnaissance of Earth. It seemed, given the statements made by hundreds of witnesses, that the creatures knew exactly what they wanted and what they were doing. This is not the uncoordinated maneuvering that had been reported in the past, but a plan that seemed to be designed down to the minor details. A plan that could be modified when the events demanded it. This moved the October 1973 wave out of the categories of the past.

In 1947 there was such a diversity of sightings that no pattern could drawn. It was the same in 1952, 1964, and 1968. Hundreds of reports or hundreds of different kinds of craft, piloted, if the aliens were reported at all, by hundreds of different kinds of aliens, doing many things that served no useful purpose. October 1973 didn't have that problem. The craft were the same, the creatures were the same and they had an easily observed purpose.

The problem with the previous waves was all the noise. That is, there was so much being reported that it tended to drown out anything that might have been good. It could be said that the Air Force, the news media, and the government contributed to the noise by continually contradicting one another, and a few people became so convinced that this meant a cover-up that they devoted their energies to finding the evidence of the cover-up rather than trying to determine the nature of the phenomena.

Important questions were entangled in the noise, important facts lost. Some researchers were no longer interested in UFO's but were investigating cases of "governmental suppression of the facts." Had the government been engineering a cover-up, they couldn't have asked for more. It diverted attention from the real problem.

Other investigators went off on other tangents. One woman spent her time asking witnesses their blood types because she was convinced that people with Rh negative blood were aliens or descendants of aliens. Another wanted only cases of black UFO's saying that these "light absorbing UFO's" might be the key to the problem.

All this is noise. All this diverts attention. Investigators began to chase the wrong cases and the wrong sightings. And, because a lot of the noise was generated by the lunatic fringe, the contactees and other such groups, that the layman, the government employees, the Air Force, and the general public, developed an unwarranted opinion of the phenomena.

The news media, wanting to capitalize on a good story, printed a lot of things about UFO's that came from the lunatic fringe. George Adamski's story of trips to Venus made good newspaper copy, but it didn't add any credibility to the UFO phenomena. The story of little bodies stored. at Wright-Patterson Air Force Base might make a good TV story, but most people realized that it wasn't true because the original story was an admitted hoax. Just more noise to confuse and confound.

The noise began to get the majority of the newspaper and TV attention. This undermined the whole phenomena so that the October 1973 reports were thought to be more examples of this. The reason people didn't recognize the importance of the October 1973 wave was the noise. This wasn't the first time that dozens of UFO's had been seen in a relatively small geographical location in a short period of time. It had all happened before. At least we thought that it had all happened before.

The first question that comes to mind, then, is where did all this nonsense about extraterrestrial spacecraft come from if not the reports of UFO's? If it wasn't true, what was there that could start such a myth? These things just don't spring into existence. The first place to look is science fiction. During the thirties, science fiction was in its heyday. Hundreds of stories were published, thousands of ideas discussed. A good example of science fiction's influence is the atomic bomb. When the first one was exploded in 1945, there were two thousand scientists who understood what had happened and there were five hundred thousand science fiction readers who understood the concept. Atomic energy had been introduced in science fiction in the thirties. It was an old stand-by in 1945.

There was another early science fiction story that led a trend. The 1930s story entitled, "The Little Green Man" was about a visitor from another planet who happened to be small and green. When people began reporting UFO's and their occupants, it was almost natural that someone would remember that story and tag all UFO occupants as little green men. And, of course, there was Orson Welles and his 1938 broadcast of "War of the Worlds." The public reaction to it was so immediate and so irrational, it's almost impossible to believe that it happened. And the question that comes to mind is what would have been the reaction in 1973 if people hadn't been conditioned by the Welles' broadcast? But the point is, people were ready to believe in spaceships and aliens so that when Kenneth Arnold made his report of nine flying saucers, there wasn't much of a gap to leap. A month later a new story surfaced to underscore the extraterrestrial nature of the phenomena.

Throughout the 1950's, magazine writers produced hundreds of articles claiming that flying saucers were real and from another world. When the Air Force or the government said that there was no evidence of extraterrestrial visits, the UFO investigators and the general public would shout, "Cover-up! Cover-up!"

And, since there was no concrete evidence for the existence of the extraterrestrial spacecraft, another large group screamed in a loud voice, "Hoax!"

All these factions added to the din. The unfortunate thing is, prior to 1973, the elimination of the noise would have eliminated all the UFO reports. This is where we run into the first divergence between 1973 and the rest of the UFO field.

It all boils down to this. In 1947, the American public was ready to believe in extraterrestrial spacecraft. They had been conditioned by nearly a half century of achievement in flight, discussions of rockets to the moon and the planets of the Solar System, and by science fiction that postulated everything from friendly visitation to invasion.

This evolution can be seen by reading the original newspaper clippings about the Great Airship of 1897. While there were a number of reports where occupants were reported, nine times out of ten, they were human. Not humanoid but human. One man claimed he talked to the crew who said they were on their way to Cuba to bomb the Spanish. Another man said that he was told that the crew was from Iowa and they would soon reveal their invention to the world. The one report of alien creatures, that is, Alexander Hamilton's report from Le Roy, Kansas, has been discovered to be a hoax. Fifty years later, the assumption wasn't for Earthly invention but for an extraterrestrial creation.

By October 1973, the factions had had twenty-six years to choose up sides. Each side said, "Here we go again." The difference was that one side knew that we were being visited, and the other knew that we weren't. Noise had convinced both sides.

The question is, then, how would we have reacted had the first UFO report been made in October 1973? There would naturally have been a period of disbelief, but how long would it have lasted? Possibly by the second week of the wave, with the reports coming fast and furious, rather than arguing whether or not there were spaceships, we would have been trying to design methods of contacting them.

We have seen how the October 1973 wave differed. We have seen how it was a time when it appeared aliens were gathering samples, information, and studying the human race. They weren't just zipping around the skies daring us to chase them, but landing with a purpose in mind. To understand how this could have happened, we must first understand the historical perspective that supposedly adds so much weight to the proof for the existence of UFO's. When that examination is completed, we will be left with very few actual UFO sightings and it is then that we will understand the significance of the October Scenario.

Part III
The Historical Perspective

FROM
ANCIENT ASTRONAUTS
TO THE GREAT AIRSHIP

In almost every book written about UFO's, a chapter or two deals with the past sightings, showing that the phenomena is not a modern one. The contention is that by adding the weight of centuries to the brief period of the modern era, we can prove that UFO's exist. To take the concept a step farther, it can be proved that UFO's are extraterrestrial spacecraft.

These books talk of fiery chariots and flaming spears claiming that the ancients didn't have sufficient vocabulary to convey an exact description of a flying saucer. They point to a medieval painting showing a flaming object shooting across the sky that has a man crouched in it, and shout that the ancients were more honest in their interpretation of their world. Here is proof that medieval scholars knew that visitors from space had landed.

These same people point to the Bible and talk of Ezekiel and the wheel. They say that this is a description of a spacecraft seen by Ezekiel and the talk of four faces and wheels within wheels is his way of describing the thing from another world. We are also told that the ancient astronauts landed dozens of times during the climb of civilization and that they gave the Egyptians, the Mayans, the Olmecs, and the Inca the information needed to forge those societies.

We are told that the statues on Easter Island are outside the range of the people who lived there, and must be the creation of a race of supermen from space. Also in this vein we are told that the Great Pyramid was not built by the Egyptians but instead created by space travelers. Further, the Plains of Nasca in Peru were designed and laid out, not by the Incas but rather by creatures from another world.

And even our pre-history is not immune to the clamor that UFO's have touched the Earth. There are stories of machined cubes or iron nails or silver vessels found in solid rock. By using one standard method of archaeological dating, it would mean that these artifacts are several hundred thousand years, or several million years old.

More proof that someone, or something, walked the Earth long before the human race had swung down from the trees.

The weight of all this information is staggering and it is a paradox that it is only the unenlightened and the scientist who refuse to see the truth. Flying saucers in ancient times is a fact, according to many of these writers and researchers. It can't be proven directly because the people who witnessed the events are long dead, but it can be deduced from the artifacts, the drawings, the writings and the paintings that they left.

Even as late as the Nineteenth Century people saw flying saucers, or in this case, a cigar-shaped craft, visiting our planet. Hundreds of sightings of the mysterious craft were made around the United States in 1897. Newspapers recorded the event and modern researchers have only recently come to appreciate the size of the wave from March and April, 1897.

The stories are all good. Unfortunately, it seems that most of them are based on rumor, hearsay, misrepresentations and out and out lies. The people writing books about UFO's take everything they can to prove their points, but rarely check any of the source material. If they did, a lot of the misinformation that is being printed as the truth would drop out of circulation.

The first area that can be eliminated here, is the descriptions of fiery chariots. Those kinds of descriptions tell us absolutely nothing. In a time when meteors and comets were not understood, and when it was believed that the sun and the moon were dragged across the heavens in some kind of chariot, it is small wonder that some of the rarer astronomical phenomena would be described as fiery or flaming. After all, what would a meteor plunging through the sky look like. Certainly it could be called some kind of plane crash, if the ancients had known about planes. They described the event in terms they had at hand. They didn't mean to convey the idea that they believed that it was something from outer space. In many cases they didn't understand the concept of outer space. They just believed that the gods were driving the meteor. That belief doesn't work today because we know what a meteor is, and yet dozens of the brightest meteors have been labeled UFO's by the modern world.

A case in point. Not long after the movie CLOSE ENCOUNTERS OF THE THIRD KIND hit the circuit, a local TV station reported a close encounter of the first kind, a sighting of a glowing shape that shot through the sky lighting up the countryside. They interviewed an amateur astronomer who said that he had never seen anything like it. It was just impossible to believe. The UFO was a meteor: A dozen other sources confirmed the fact. Newspapers the next day headlined the fireball that had lit up the state. There was no longer a question as to the identity of the UFO. I wondered why the TV station had interviewed an amateur astronomer when Doctor James A. van Allen taught at the university only thirty miles away.

The point is, even in the modern world, peopled by individuals who are supposed to know better, we are fooled. An amateur astronomer couldn't identify a meteor because the colors were different than any he had seen before. A rare event, but not a spacecraft.

The meteor and comet are also responsible for the painting in the medieval church. Even in those times it was believed that someone had to be controlling the meteor because no one knew what they were. They had seen nothing to suggest that someone had to be inside, they just believed it, so when the daylight meteor flashed through the sky above them, they added the man to their drawing of it. They added the picture of the "lesser god" or angel who had to be inside, based on no observational data whatsoever.

So, we can eliminate the descriptions of fiery chariots and flaming spears. They add too little to our knowledge, and the interpretation of those statements are open to a wide range of conclusions, the least likely being spacecraft.

But that doesn't answer the specific questions. There are, according to many, including Erich von Daniken, too many things in the ancient world that can't be explained by modern science. The pyramids, a metal pillar in India that doesn't rust, the statues of Easter Island, the super societies of Mexico and South America that were far advanced. These things prove that there were flying saucers in ancient times because there is no other explanation for them.

The theories are interesting but most are not based on fact. The authors have latched onto some rather poor evidence and built a structure that is weakly supported. They attempt to strengthen their theories by making ridiculous, and often false claims about the current state of archaeology. We will examine some of the theories and attempt to find a thread of truth and logic in them.

Von Daniken dealt with the civilization of Meso-America and the Central Andes in the course of his works on ancient astronauts. Scientists having studied that area, or who are trained in Egyptian history, or any field of pre-history, can punch holes in von Daniken's theories. There will not be explanations for all the "strange" artifacts found on Earth because such explanations don't always exist. The point is that many explanations can be made inside our current knowledge without having to invent ancient astronauts.

It's almost impossible to decide where to begin. There are so many inaccuracies and half-truths, but we will try to start where von Daniken did by discussing the Mayans. He, of course, refers to their accurate calendar and their almost supernatural knowledge of astronomy. No one denies that the Mayans were advanced in those areas. The dispute centers on the source of the knowledge.

Von Daniken points out that the Mayans knew about the planets Uranus and Neptune, both "discovered" by western scientists only after the invention of the telescope. This was, of course, an exceptional piece of knowledge for the Mayans to have, but nowhere completely out of the ordinary. It is possible that the Mayans were able to discover both planets themselves. The knowledge is not suggestive of space travelers as von Daniken would have us believe, because the knowledge is not complete.

If there were travelers from space, why is there no mention of the last planet, Pluto? Why is there no mention of the satellites of Jupiter or the fantastic rings of Saturn? Why no mention of the tiny moons of Mars or the dimmer rings of Jupiter, Uranus and Neptune? These are facts that require the knowledge of the telescope to see, or an ability to send out space probes, and a technology that was out of bounds for the Mayans. Space travelers, the gods from outer space, would have known these things and they would have given that knowledge to the Mayans, just as they had given them the knowledge of Uranus and Neptune. Had there been any space travelers to give out that knowledge.

Von Daniken, after showing the knowledge of the Mayans, claims that they abandoned their city, "overnight" and moved 220 miles to the north. The clues to his mistake are the idea that the Mayans abandoned the city overnight, and that they never returned. Both ideas are inaccurate. However, to prove the point, we have to refer to modern archaeology, a "mistake" that von Daniken makes only when he needs to bolster a point.

96

Evidence indicates that the abandonment took place over several years. The reasons for it are still unknown. The effects of their leaving was like an overnight evacuation when compared to the slowly dwindling populations in other areas. But it was not that the Mayans lived there one day and were gone the next. And, not the whole population disappeared. Again, there is evidence that, at the very least, part of the priest class used the city for years. The other Mayans may not have been allowed to return, but someone continued to live there.

Some of his other claims about ancient American civilizations are as inaccurate. At one point, when discussing the Inca roads, he asked, "Of what use are roads that run parallel to each other? That intersect? That are laid out in a plain and come suddenly to an end?"

The questions are almost too ridiculous to answer. Have you ever heard of an interstate highway? Roads that run parallel. How many street corners did you pass going to work or to the store or to school? Roads that intersect.

The last part of the question is the hardest to answer but it can be done. First, every city has a number of dead end streets. Roads that go nowhere, except to a few houses or to an out of the way business. Second, because the road leads nowhere today doesn't mean it didn't lead anywhere a thousand years ago. There is a Roman road that leads to the sea and abruptly stops. Modern science has discovered that it crosses what was once dry land and re-emerges on the other side. It is, however, a road that leads nowhere.

Other authors have followed von Daniken's example. They have grabbed anything and everything that remotely resembles a technological achievement in ancient times and claimed that it could not be the result of an idea by the people living at that time. For example, one man made quite a deal out of the batteries that were found in ancient Babylon, making the point that the Babylonians had no need for the batteries, and therefore, the batteries do not belong to them but to space travelers.

Anthropology can explain the batteries, without the benefit of space travelers and gods from outer space. First, however, it should be pointed out that the batteries are not the closed, stored energy, flashlight cells that we have today, but crude ones that barely created a current. In fact, many kids have made similar batteries in grade school science lab. All you need is a lemon, two pieces of metal and a length of wire. Put them together correctly and you can generate a current. The Babylonian batteries were basically the same low level technology.

97

Consider that the anthropological law stating that whenever the cultural elements exist for an invention, it will be invented. Babylon had metal alloys, lemons and wire. They could "invent" the battery. They had no use for it and the invention was forgotten. There are hundreds of examples of this, but only a few have been attributed to gods from outer space.

Hero, the ancient Egyptian, invented the steam engine. An application for the engine should have been easily seen, but Hero never pursued it. One of the reasons was the slave society in Egypt. They didn't need "labor saving" devices because they had slaves to do the labor. The cultural need for the engine didn't exist but the cultural elements, or parts, did. No one has yet claimed that Hero was given the engine by ancient astronauts.

One author included several pictures of the statues at Tiahuanaco because the eyes were oval, square, or round, but not slanted. He claimed that this proved the theory about a land bridge and the Asian origin of the American Indians to be wrong. He didn't explain the significance of the other statues with their square mouths and feline features.

We can use the author's logic against him, a trick that he is careful to warn us about. We are not supposed to think about his ideas, only accept them. One of the most prevalent of the motifs of the statues built in the ancient American civilizations was the jaguar. There was a cult of "were-jaguars" and their priests fostered the belief in them. Many statues show the feline motif and if we believe that the artists were only sculpting what they saw, then we must accept the were-jaguars. There must really have been a group that really could change themselves into jaguars.

Of course, that overlooks the possibility that the artists had a certain amount of imagination. He may have been representing what he believed the were jaguars looked like. Statues, no matter what they look like, do not prove that the artist was accurately reproducing anything. Before accepting one point of view, we must be aware of all the facts and not just part of them.

Those authors have harped on many of the achievements of ancient humans, saying, with no justification, that the human race was not able to create those marvels. They have not proved their case. They have only caused more trouble for the honest researcher. Anytime that something hits it big, as did the ancient astronauts theory, there are dozens of imitations. But sheer weight doesn't make the case.

That is one of the points that should be made here. None of the information or facts used by von Daniken or the others, proves, or even leads to the necessity of having ancient astronauts. Earth people could easily have had the knowledge to do the impossible things.

For example, the ancient Greeks had all sorts of knowledge that has only recently been rediscovered. They knew the size of the Earth to a very accurate degree, and didn't need space travelers to tell them the dimensions. Their work with geometry gave them the answer. They had atomic theories, and understood the workings of the solar system. They didn't have a government or religion that forced them to look the other way, and that is why they continued to advance.

The Dark Ages, the church, and the lack of education, took some of that knowledge away from us. But we had obtained it on our own. The Greeks and Romans and Incas and Aztecs were able to observe nature and to learn from it. They didn't need ancient astronauts to bestow the information upon them.

So one might ask, "If there were ancient astronauts, why have they stopped teaching? " Why aren't they around now that we really need them? Did the human race do something that alienated them, or are they trying to teach us a lesson? That is the big fault in all the ancient astronaut theories. Where are they now that we could really use their help?"

Of course, you can always point to the Aztecs or Mayans and say that they described people that they had never seen. Why were the Aztecs, among others, fooled by Cortez, if ancient astronauts hadn't been around?

There is, again, an answer. In fact, a little research by those proponents of the ancient astronauts would have given them the answer. When the Spanish arrived in Meso-America, they were greeted by two Spanish sailors. They had been shipwrecked years earlier, and had been rescued by the Mayans. Traditions suggested that it had happened before. A ship, badly damaged and blown off course had landed in South America. Of course, the men who had survived had knowledge superior to that of the natives who found them. By carefully using that knowledge, they could have convinced some that they were gods.

By the same token, evidence does exist that shows that Japanese fishermen or explorers have reached the western coast of Meso-America. The evidence isn't very good and is dubious, but it makes more sense than aliens from space. And the evidence is improving every day.

Easter Island provided us with another example of this pseudo science gone mad. Von Daniken and the others claim that the people living on the island had no way to build those stone gods that line the edges of the island. They didn't have the tools, the knowledge, or the society to do it. The claim is that the statues were ancient when the people arrived. They were built by someone other than the inhabitants of the island.

All this is untrue. We know when the statues were built, we know who built them, we know how they were built, and we know why the building of them stopped. Hardly a mystery. Yet von Daniken and his cult of followers overlook all that information.

According to science, at the time the statues were built, there were two groups living on the island. One group originated the statues as a way of pleasing their god, and making sure that they would receive bountiful gifts. The other group followed suit. Both groups built statues until the social order began to collapse. The civil war that resulted led to the elimination of one of the groups. But the war had so badly affected the island that no new statues were built. That is, until Thor Heyerdahl asked the "mayor" of the island how it was done.

The explanation was simple. Using the tools that von Daniken claimed were inadequate, six men carved a huge statue from the rock quarry that von Daniken said they couldn't use. They transported the statue across the island using wooden rollers, and then using a lever system, a deep pit, and hundreds of stones, they erected the statue. All done in front of Heyerdahl without the need of extraterrestrial assistance.

And all this leads right back to the Egyptians. Von Daniken, among others, has said that the Egyptians didn't have the technical knowledge to build the pyramids. They claim that the pyramid is something that "sprang into existence" almost overnight. There are no examples of pyramids that show an evolution to the Great Pyramid.

And, again, the information is all wrong. First, there are examples of pyramid evolution. The Pyramid at Meidum shows walls that collapsed, probably because the sides were too steep. The Pyramid at Dahshur is bent, almost as if the collapse of the earlier pyramid had told the builders what to expect. They changed the design to prevent another disaster.

I pointed this out to a class of high school students who wanted to learn more about flying saucers. I was suggesting that someone should ask a few questions of those who believed in ancient astronauts. It was fashionable to ridicule science but not those making the outrageous claims.

One of the students wanted to take exception to what I said. I told him to go ahead because this was a discussion of ideas, something that von Daniken and his followers tried to avoid. The student claimed that the Egyptians would have needed five million pieces of rope to complete the Great Pyramid. He said that their technology wouldn't allow them to produce that much rope.

I agreed that it might just be a valid point. But. How long is a piece of rope? To me, finding five million pieces of rope twenty feet long would be twice as hard as finding five million pieces of rope ten feet long. All they needed for that was to find two and a half million pieces of rope twenty feet long and then cut them all in half. I also asked the student if he was aware that the remains of the rope had been found in the sand surrounding the Great Pyramid. Physical evidence that could be tested and not idle speculation by a man who hadn't completed his homework.

It appeared to me that we had looked at a lot of mysteries, done a little research and discovered that the case for the ancient astronauts was not quite as convincing as we had been led to believe. There were holes large enough to sail aircraft carriers through. Hardly the airtight case that von Daniken claimed that any thinking individual would find.

Without more evidence, the ancient astronaut theory dies. Ockham's Razor takes care of it. Why postulate space when it isn't needed to answer the question? Obviously you don't. There were no ancient astronauts.

So, it is possible that ancients of the human race built the pyramids and statues and the cities that they are credited with building. But what about the out of place artifacts? The prime example of this is the silver vessel that supposedly came from solid rock. We are to believe the story because the source quoted is an 1851 edition of the SCIENTIFIC AMERICAN. It is considered to be the finest of the out of place artifact stories.

According to modern sources, the SCIENTIFIC AMERICAN story claims, "...powerful blast was made in rock at Meeting House Hill, in Dorchester...The blast threw an immense amount of rock...and scattered small fragments in all directions...Among them was...a metallic vessel in two parts...putting the two parts together it formed a bell-shaped vessel...The chasing, a carving and inlaying are exquisitely done...This curious and unknown vessel was blown out of the pudding stone fifteen feet below the surface...the matter is worthy of investigation, as there is no deception."

Copies of the SCIENTIFIC AMERICAN for 1851 are not that hard to find. Almost any large university library will have thousands of bound periodicals going back into the Eighteenth Century, so the relatively recent 1851 editions are there. I spent an afternoon reading the SCIENTIFIC AMERICAN, but found no reference to any kind of silver vessel being blasted out of rock. I tried the index and found several curiosities listed, but none for the metal vessel. I tried several years, thinking that the writer of the first article might have misread the numbers, but failed to find any reference. I can only conclude that the item is a hoax. A hoax that has been mentioned in a dozen or more UFO books, but a hoax. An out of place artifact that doesn't exist.

Another example of this is the road that Tom Kenny of Plateau Springs, Colorado found in 1936, while excavating a cellar. Since no one would build a road underground, it was suggested that someone in Earth's ancient past had built it, and the movement of the Earth's surface, the blowing winds and weathering, covered the road for thousands of years, until Kenny found it.

I wrote to the Plateau Springs, Colorado Chamber of Commerce and asked them about the road. Apparently they don't think that it is as strange as the ancient astronaut writer thought it was. In fact, the impression that I received was that the road was part of a shallow lake bed that had dried up long before. When the clay like bottom began to dry, it cracked and split and hardened. Anyone in a drought area has seen the same thing. This was the remains of a drought in the past.

The point here is that the pavement that Kenny found could have been caused by a devastating drought that hit the region in 1077 A.D. Instead of rainfall filling the lake, blowing sand and dirt did. It gives the impression of pavement but it is something that was caused by nature and not built by the gods from outer space.

Other examples of the out of place artifacts also vanish under research. The facts of their discovery are misinterpreted. The dates given for them are totally out of line. The abilities of the ancient people are badly underestimated. Or another hoax is added to the files. Out of place artifacts don't prove alien intervention. They only prove that a large number of people are guilty of poor research techniques.

The same thing can be said about the Great Airship. This was a craft that supposedly appeared in the skies over mid-America at the end of the Nineteenth Century. Like our modern UFO waves, this was a period of intense activity. In fact, some researchers have labeled it as the first UFO wave. An examination of it, a serious study of it, gives us a new picture of it.

The first reports were at best, sketchy. On March 29, 1897, the airship was seen over Omaha, Nebraska. At the same time, and to the east, a cigar-shaped craft was chasing a farmer near Sioux City, Iowa. Robert Hubbard said that he was riding his bicycle and hoping to see the airship "that the whole country is talking about." An "anchor" was being dragged along the ground by the airship and it snagged Hubbard, hauling him off his feet. Suddenly, and "none too soon," his pants gave up the fight and with a loud ripping sound, Hubbard fell back to the ground. Although he was physically unhurt, he was angry. He told reporters that it was "criminal for the skipper of the ship to let a grapnel drag along the ground."

The next night, the citizens of Denver, Colorado saw it, and on April 1, the aerial cigar was over Kansas City, Kansas. Hundreds of people in and around the city said they saw the ship as it paused from time to time to play with its searchlight. About an hour later, the airship was seen near Everest, Kansas. Witnesses said that the cigar had wings and glowed brightly while hovering.

With all thoughts of April Fool's Day gone, the residents of Decatur, Michigan saw the airship on April 2, 1897. According to the story, the first evidence of the airship was an extremely bright light. Behind the light, a dark shape could be seen from which a sharp crackling sound and voices could be heard.

On April 10, the airship was in Illinois. From Chicago, thousands watched an airship displaying its lights. Later the same evening the aerial apparition made at least one landing. As the cigar descended toward a field near Carlinville, Illinois, a crowd began to gather. It settled into a pasture and the curious started forward. Apparently the crew thought the Earthlings too close and the ship took off. At the same time, it was also being seen in several Iowa towns. Clinton reported it first, then Ottumwa and Albia.

Two nights later, the flying panatella was again on the ground. According to the witnesses, the object was large, cigar shaped, with wings and a canopy over the top. A man climbed out, walked around as if looking for damage. After fifteen minutes, the airship "rose to a great height," and disappeared to the north. On the same evening, an engineer on a train near Chicago said he watched the airship for several minutes but "was forced to turn my attention back to my duties." When he looked up again, the airship was far ahead of the train and near Lisle, Illinois, he lost sight of it.

On April 14, there was a series of landings in Iowa. The Cedar Rapids Evening Gazette reported that the giant cigar landed on the Union Station in the "wee morning" hours and that several local citizens were taken on board. Charley Jordan quickly made his story known and even signed an affidavit attesting to his flight. He was described as "never telling a lie but a few times and then only about things of importance." Also taken for a flight was W.R. Boyd, whose whole purpose in going was to "get as high as possible so that he could learn about the condition of the post office." The members of the strange crew were very tired from their journey but promised to lecture about their trip quite soon. The topics to be discussed included the unlikely subject of Hell.

Near Cedar Rapids and also on the Cedar River is Waterloo. The night after the Cedar Rapids report, the airship was captured in Waterloo. The Waterloo Courier said that the unusual craft "came to rest on the fair ground," and one of the pilots went to the police station to ask that they guard the ship. Arriving at the fair grounds, the police were confronted with a large, twin-cigar-shaped object. All during the day people came to see the ship, the first tangible object to be found and that made the story a little more plausible.

A heavily accented "professor" from San Francisco told of the dangerous flight across country that ended in tragedy when the leader of the expedition fell into the Cedar River. The "ship" was finally removed from the fair grounds after hundreds had had the chance to see it.

In Texas, they still were not satisfied. A man in Denton saw the airship and said that it was definitely some "kind of manufactured craft."

April 17 is loaded with airship stories. Early in the morning two men from Rhome, Texas, said that they saw the giant cigar heading west at a hundred and fifty miles an hour. The same day, the Fort Worth Register, which "hardly cares to repeat it" reported that a man traveling near Cisco, Texas, saw the airship in a field. Several men were standing around and Patrick Barnes went over to talk to them. At the ship he was told they had engine trouble, but would be leaving soon to go to Cuba to bomb the Spanish. By one o'clock the craft was repaired and they took off for the Ozarks to train for their mission.

In Paris, Texas, a night watchman said that he saw the cigar shaped craft that was two hundred feet long and that had large wings. Later, in Farmersville, several people said they heard the crew of an airship singing hymns.

April 17, 1897, dawned quietly in Aurora, Texas. By the time the sun had risen, everyone in Aurora was up and starting the new day. At six, near the southern horizon, the Great Airship appeared. Texans have a thing about not being outdone and where the ship•had only landed in Iowa and Illinois, it blew up in Texas. Not only did it blow up once, but many times in many locations. But, in all fairness, Aurora is said to have originated the exploding cigar.

The airship came in low and buzzed the town square. It continued north and on the farm of Judge Proctor it hit a windmill. There was an explosion and the Great Airship disintegrated. Damage was done to the judge's flower garden and his house and people rushed to the wreck. They found the dead pilot, his body badly disfigured. "He was not of this Earth," said T.J. Weems, a Signal Corps officer. He thought the man probably came from Mars.

Searchers found several documents covered with a strange writing. It is claimed the airship weighed several tons and was made of silver and aluminum. By noon of the seventeenth, all the debris had been cleaned up. Apparently no one in Aurora had anything else to do, so late in the afternoon, they gave the Martian a Christian burial.

On April 19, the airship briefly left Texas and was near Sisterville, West Virginia. Residents of the nearby hills said they could see a large cigar behind the flashing multi-colored lights. A lone man in El Paso, Texas, reported the airship on the nineteenth. Light showed through the portholes, there were several lights at both ends and he said that he could hear voices but couldn't tell what language they were speaking. The ship disappeared in the south over Mexico. On April 20, the airship was seen in Longview, Texas.

One of the strangest stories came from LeRoy, Kansas on April 21. About 10:30 on Monday night, Alexander Hamilton and his son were awakened by noise among the cattle. Running outside, he was surprised to see an aerial object above his cowpen. From the glowing red ship he saw a rope that was looped around the head of one of his heifers. The cow was caught in the fence and was being pulled off its feet toward the ship. Attempts to cut the rope failed and instead, Hamilton cut the wire fence, freeing the calf. The airship, calf and all, then disappeared into the night sky.

The next evening, Link Thomas arrived at the Hamilton ranch. He had found the remains of a cow bearing Hamilton's brand and although the ground near the calf was soft there were no footprints. It was as if the cow had been dropped from the sky. Hamilton signed an affidavit attesting to his experiences. Several of the town's prominent citizens signed a statement saying they knew Hamilton and believed him. Hamilton was later elected to the state legislature.

Toward the end of April, the airship returned to Texas. On April 22, in Josserand, Frank Nichols said he was awakened by a whirring noise like that of machinery. On the ground in his cornfield was the aerial contrivance. Outside, two men with buckets asked Nichols for permission to use his well. Before they took off, the crew told Nichols they were from Iowa and in a few weeks would reveal their invention. One long time resident of San Angelo, Texas, reported he saw the airship fly into a flock of birds and explode. Once again, the mystery craft was claimed to have been destroyed.

One of the final reports came a few days following that destruction. Dozens of people returning from church saw the ship, its anchor fouled in a barbed wire fence. Climbing down a rope was a small man in a blue sailor suit. When he saw the crowd watching, he cut the anchor loose and scurried back to the cigar. The people cut the anchor free and it was on display for weeks in Merkel, Texas.

That's the story of the Great Airship or rather that's it with a minimum of research. Most of the cases are impressive, sensational and even astonishing. Some researchers have completed their investigations right there but further work reveals much more about the stories.

The first evidence of a hoax is found in the Cedar Rapids, Iowa report. The men there stopped telling their story and quietly gave the spotlight to the "scientists" in Waterloo. The Cedar Rapids men only had their story but in Waterloo, they had the airship. Hundreds flocked to the fairgrounds to see the object and it remained there for days. Finally, one of the German professors was recognized as E.A. Feather, a local man and the hoax was exposed. They admitted it, everyone had a good laugh and the junk was removed from the fairgrounds.

Some of the stories, such as the men talking to the airship pilots don't deserve much more attention or research. For example, the crew of an airship saying they were on the way to Cuba to bomb the Spanish indicates a hoax. At least they never dropped any bombs and weren't heard from again. Nichols and his story of the Iowa airship is not very important either. The airship crew said that they would soon reveal their invention and the fact that they didn't indicates that it too, was a hoax.

Aurora, Texas, provided the most sensational case. Dozens of UFO investigators have seized upon the story, researching it, checking the graveyard for the dead pilot's headstone, searching Proctor's farm with metal detectors, and even making a grandstand play by trying to have the "Martian's" body exhumed. Once again, good research would have burst the balloon.

H.E. Hayden was a stringer for the Dallas newspaper and had sent the Aurora crash story to the Dallas Morning News. They printed it as they had printed several other airship stories during that week. Hayden apparently saw an opportunity to put his town back on the map. He missed by seventy years.

The story, however, breaks down rapidly. T.J. Weems was not a member of the Signal Corps, but the local blacksmith. Residents of Aurora since 1897 (and when I checked out this story in 1972, there were several still living there) claimed that they knew nothing about the airship crash. And although Judge Proctor did own a farm in Aurora, he didn't have a windmill. (At least, the present owner of the land said that in 1969, but now, with all the publicity about the crash, he claims that Proctor had two wells and one did have a windmill.) The final blow comes from Hayden himself. He finally admitted to making up the story in an attempt to draw people and attention to Aurora.

Recent attempts to revitalize the story have had little success. Metal found in Aurora and sent to a Canadian lab didn't turn out to be anything strange. Other proof of the crash vanished in the light of good research. The Wise County Historical Society (Aurora is located in Wise County) said that nothing like that had ever happened. One member did say, "I wish we could prove that it did happen, but it didn't."

When many reports begin to breakdown, similar cases became suspect. Alexander Hamilton's LeRoy, Kansas, sighting did contain signed affidavits claiming that he had seen the airship and claiming that he was an honest man. But the affidavits mean nothing because it was discovered that Hamilton, along with all the other affidavit signers belonged to the local liars club. They were all parties to the hoax. Hamilton's daughter revealed the truth about it in the late 1960's.

The next question is, "How did the whole mess start?" Was there something in the beginning, some strange airship that everyone wanted to see or was it a giant prank that everyone helped to perpetuate? The answers are found in a report by the Des Moines Register in 1897. Before answering the questions about the airship, the paper carried some more accounts of its activities. It's mentioned in Cedar Rapids on the fourteenth, and on the next night it was seen near Fairfield, Iowa. In fact, the airship did well that night, being seen in Evanston, Illinois and "worrying the papers greatly." The most remarkable account of the airship on April 15 was from Pella, Iowa. According to the paper, "many people, among them the Western Union operator had seen the machine." They said the airship looked just like it had been described in the papers. The report continued, "This was a neat attempt at getting around the description; if it was true, the Pella airship looked like a sea serpent, a balloon, a winged cigar, a pair of balloons hitched together with a car swung between them, a car with an aeroplane and three sails or nineteen or twenty other things."

The Register continued saying that at about 9:00 p.m. on Saturday night, the phone in the Leader (an Iowa newspaper) office rang and the town of Stuart was "found to be clamoring for fame." They had seen the airship. The story went out over the wire and the Western Union operator said that he could produce dozens of witnesses if anyone cared. He said that the airship had come from the southeast, was traveling about fifteen miles an hour and had a red light in front and a green one in the rear. The operator's feelings were hurt when he was asked if this was an April Fool's joke.

While the conversation between the newspaper and the telegrapher was becoming heated, a report came in that the airship was now over Panora, Iowa. The Western Union operator there cut in and said that they had seen the airship over their town coming from the direction of Stuart. It was now flying faster, but had the same appearance as it did in Stuart.

As the argument increased in intensity, the numbers of telegrams about the airship also increased. From Clinton, Iowa, came a message saying that the airship had flown over the town on April 10. It was seen by several reputable citizens. The telegram was almost apologetic. Immediately came a telegram from Ottumwa, Iowa, and they had seen the airship more than once. "An Eldon (Iowa) operator discovered the airship at 7:25 p.m. Ottumwa was prepared for its appearance. It was seen here by half the population. All agreed that it appeared as a red light moving up and down and traveling northwest. Albia (Iowa) caught sight of it at 8:10 and at 9:00 it was still visible...This is the third time that it has been seen in Albia."

From Burlington, Iowa, came one of the "meanest and most discouraging stories of the entire lot." Members of the Burlington newspaper staff sent up a common tissue paper hot air balloon (somewhat similar to the cleaning bag reports of today) so that it would carry over the city. The test results were satisfactory because they soon began getting calls from the citizens describing the airship. One of the most distinguished men of the town came forward to say he had seen the ship and would sign an affidavit saying that he had heard voices from it. That convinced the newspaper reporters that the whole airship episode was a fake.

The Register goes on to say, "The fact seems to be that the airship has been exploited beautifully by telegraphers along certain lines of the railroad. They managed it beautifully for awhile and never allowed it to travel too far too fast." The reports were always well done showing a certain amount of genius. But the rest of the public began to take a hand and the airship reports got too numerous. Some would conflict and it became evident that someone would have to have made a whole family of airships.

The airship idea seems to have originated in San Francisco the year before. In November, 1896, an airship with stubby wings was reported over that city. Dozens reported seeing the ship and the newspaper spread the word. The press of the entire country finally carried the story. But it was soon admitted that the airship there was a paper created hot air balloon and the newspaper was in on the joke. From the success of this first joke, the fleet of jokes was launched. The airship then appeared in Omaha, Nebraska, and it has been proved that there too, the airship was full of hot air.

It seems that everyone was willing to help the airship. The telegraphers were always willing to report the airship when it was due to be seen over their city. People with active imaginations helped supply the details. The Burlington hot air balloon seems to show that most of the airship sighters were full of hot air too.

The Register ends the account saying, "Of course, it had degenerated into something of a joke since the ship became so common: but all the same, it deserves to rank as one of the most successful fakes of an era of such successes."

With the destruction of the Great Airship, it can be said that we start the modern era with a clean slate. The evidence for past visits by spaceships or gods from outer space is not based on serious research. Up until 1947, when the modern era began, it can be said that there were no UFO's, no extraterrestrial spacecraft. There was only the human race, struggling to become great without outside intervention

.

THE MODERN ERA

The modern era began in a flurry of activity that set the stage for later years. Various investigators, some of them with official status, were thrown into the controversy in the hope of finding a quick and easy solution. When that failed, other steps were tried.

The Air Force hadn't even been created when the first UFO sighting of the modern era was splashed across the front pages of hundreds of newspapers. Kenneth Arnold landed his private plane in June, 1947, in Washington to report that he had seen what looked like nine disc shaped objects, nine "flying saucers," skipping through the air near Mount Rainier. He had never seen anything like it.

From that point the race was on. Who could come up with the best sighting the fastest? Hundreds entered the derby, a few with out of focus pictures of high flying discs. But none of them had anything conclusive. Only a month after Arnold's report two Air Force officers (in reality they were Army Air Corps officers, the Air Force wouldn't exist for six months) heard about UFO physical evidence. This was the conclusive evidence that everyone wanted and this was the sighting that would set the tone for the next several years.

On July 31, 1947, the intelligence unit at Hamilton Air Force Base, California, learned that two harbor patrolmen had recovered metal from a flying saucer. Lieutenant Frank Brown got a call from a man he had met on the Arnold investigation. Ed Ruppelt, one time head of Project Bluebook, identified the caller as an airline pilot named Simpson, but it was later learned that the caller was Kenneth Arnold himself. Because Brown knew Arnold and respected his judgment, Brown decided that he would follow the lead.

111

Within an hour, Brown, with a Captain Davidson, left California for Maury Island, near Tacoma, Washington, the site of the UFO report. Brown and Davidson met Arnold at the airport and all returned to Arnold's room for a briefing. While there, Arnold mentioned that he had received some money from a Chicago publisher for his part in the investigations. Although it was never revealed, further investigation suggests that Ray Palmer was the publisher. Arnold felt that the story was getting too big and that he should have help, so he had called the Air Force.

Arnold had heard the whole report about Maury Island but he wanted the intelligence officers to hear it firsthand. He delayed telling them any more than they already knew because he didn't want to prejudice the investigations. The two harbor patrolmen were called but they were already on their way to the hotel.

Once again, Ruppelt identified the men by using fictitious names but their real names have been published since. The men, Dahl and Crissman, along with Dahl's son and a pet dog, claimed that they had been operating in the area of Maury Island in June, 1947. It was a bleak, overcast day with a relatively low cloud cover. Everyone's attention was suddenly drawn to six, doughnut shaped objects that appeared just below the clouds. The objects dashed toward the boat, stopping only five hundred feet away.

Dahl said that he thought one of the objects was in trouble because the other five circled it. The objects were hovering so everyone got a good look at them and described them as one hundred feet in diameter with a hole twenty-five feet in diameter in the center. The surface appeared to be a bright metal and no one heard any noise or saw any type of trail behind the ships.

While the UFO's hovered, Dahl took pictures. He photographed one of the objects as it maneuvered to the disabled craft and appeared to make contact. Minutes later, when the contact was broken, there was a dull thud, and the UFO began to spit "sheets" of light metal from the hole in the center. As the metal floated down, the object began to throw off a harder, rock-like substance and this fell to the beach on Maury Island. The harbor patrolmen turned their boat toward the island and the rock-like slag fell onto the deck, damaging the boat, burning the arm of Dahl's son and killing their dog.

On the beach, the man gathered samples of the "slag" and kept an eye on the UFO's that were leaving the area at high speed. Dahl tried to radio for help but the reception was so bad that he couldn't make contact. After

112

gathering the samples, the men returned to their base, obtained first aid for the burns and reported the incident to their supervisor. The supervisor didn't believe the story until he went to the island and saw the metal. That convinced him. Both Dahl and Crissman agreed this was the whole story as it had happened.

That, however, wasn't the end of it. The next morning, Dahl claimed that a strange man, dressed in a dark suit came to visit him. The man was aware of the incident, described the scene to Dahl and suggested that he forget all about it.

Later that same day, Dahl had the pictures developed but they were badly "fogged" and spotted. One man suggested that the film had been exposed to radiation of some kind.

Next, Arnold said that he had problems with mysterious callers and tipsters. Somehow the Tacoma newspaper was getting a great deal of information about the discussions going on in his hotel room. If none of the men in the room were leaking the story, how was the paper finding out about it? Arnold, with help, made a thorough search of the room and found no hidden microphone. He was completely baffled.

Brown and Davidson didn't stay long after hearing the story. They asked a few questions and tried to leave. Dahl and Crissman offered some of the metal but Brown was reluctant to take it. Some have claimed that Brown knew the story was a hoax at that point and didn't want to become more involved. He had recognized the metal as slag.

Brown and Davidson returned to McChord Air Force Base (Washington) and while waiting for their plane, told the intelligence officer there that they thought the story was a hoax. Quickly, they outlined why they felt that way but were reluctant to talk about it, feeling that the Air Force had already wasted too much time on the case. It was a good thing that they did talk to the intelligence officer at McChord, because, a few hours later, they were both dead in a plane crash.

Newspapers hinted that the plane had been sabotaged and that it was carrying classified material. The hint was that the classified material was the case file and metal samples from Maury Island. That is not true. Classified material was on the plane but it had nothing to do with UFO's.

Later, there were reports that the harbor patrolmen disappeared. Ed Ruppelt suggested that they should have disappeared, "right into Puget Sound." He said that Maury Island was possibly the dirtiest hoax in UFO history mainly because it cost the lives of two men.

The official report on Maury Island claimed that it was a hoax from the very beginning. Both Dahl and Crissman later admitted that the rock fragments had nothing to do with UFO's. They had said that the rocks were from UFO's because that was what the Chicago publisher wanted to hear. They had written to the man, (Palmer) enclosing a small piece of rock. They had done it as a joke but it had snowballed on them. Palmer then called Arnold and asked him to investigate.

Neither man could ever produce the photographs. That, of course, makes the case very shaky. If they had pictures of six UFO's, they would have taken care to protect them but both men said that the pictures had been misplaced. They never said that they had been stolen, only lost.

One of the men, Dahl or Crissman, was the mysterious caller to the newspapers. That was how the Tacoma paper had found out what was happening behind closed doors. If the story was true, Dahl and Crissman wouldn't need to leak parts of it for publicity. In a few Days they would have been very famous.

And, they were not harbor patrolmen. They owned a couple of beat up salvage boats and worked the sound looking for floating lumber. That also ruled out part of their story and destroyed their credibility. The airplane crash was just that - an aircraft accident. An engine had caught fire and a wing came off. It hadn't been "shot" down by UFO's to prevent the men from reporting. If that had been the purpose, the UFO failed. The box of fragments forced on Brown was recovered from the wreckage of the plane.

Brown and Davidson had smelled the hoax from the beginning and had gotten out as fast as possible, after they confirmed it. That was the reason they didn't want the fragments. They were afraid they would inadvertently lend a note of credibility to the story. You've seen the headlines before: AIR FORCE OFFICERS TAKE MYSTERY SAMPLE." At McChord, an unidentified informer had already told the intelligence officer that the metal was worthless slag, which confirmed what Brown had believed.

Brown and Davidson didn't tell Arnold about the hoax because he had been so thoroughly taken. It is understandable and doesn't reflect on him. If anything is to be said about Arnold's handling of the investigation, it should be good. He had the sense to call in others when he found himself in over his head. It may have been a disservice on the parts of Brown and Davidson for not telling him when they simply didn't want to embarrass him.

The final point, the one that convinces some that Maury Island wasn't a hoax is that neither Dahl nor Crissman were prosecuted for inventing the sighting. Air Force records show that it was considered, seriously considered. In fact, an investigation was made to determine whether or not the government had a case. The outcome was that neither man had wanted to cause trouble, but the story had snowballed. It had started as a harmless joke. The deaths of the two officers and the loss of the plane was not directly caused by the story and nothing would be accomplished by prosecuting Dahl and Crissman.

The last chapter to the Maury Island story was written months after it had begun. Air Force officers, to keep from prejudicing their case while they were considering prosecution, did not leak any information about the hoax. They withheld it. When it was finally released, it was old news, and almost no one reads yesterday's papers. The public was left with the mistaken belief that the Air Force had no answers for the story.

As the official investigation found the solution to the Maury Island case, it was realized by higher authorities that more than a haphazard investigation was needed. Project Sign was created in January 1948 and headquartered at Wright-Patterson Air Force Base in Dayton, Ohio.

Sign investigated many of the UFO reports that were to become classics in the field. Later Project Sign officers were asked to present an estimate of the situation. Their conclusion was that UFO's were spacecraft from another planet. General Hoyt S. Vandenburg, the Air Force Chief of Staff said that the evidence didn't support the conclusion and he rejected the report. Supposedly all copies of the report, which had been classified Top Secret, were destroyed.

With that slap in the face, the life seeped out of the project. Its name was changed to Grudge in 1949. There was an attempt to investigate sightings, but the opinion of the staff was that there wasn't anything to them. In the end, almost nothing was being done.

In 1951, the officers at the Air Technical Intelligence Center, which controlled Grudge, were asked what was happening in the UFO field. When someone said, "About nothing," the project's name was changed again, and it was revitalized as "Bluebook."

During the next seventeen years, the emphasis on UFO's changed. Under Ruppelt, Bluebook's first director, a serious effort was made to examine the

UFO reports reaching Ohio. Under later directors, Bluebook became a clearinghouse for public information. And the public wasn't happy with the information it was receiving. They felt that something interesting must be happening because the Air Force was continuing to classify UFO reports.

A prime example of this is the Air Force investigation of the photos taken in August 1965 by Rex Heflin. Air Force investigators concluded that the pictures were fakes. The Condon Committee dismissed them because there were "many internal inconsistencies in them." Nearly everyone else believed the photos to be among the best ever taken.

Heflin was a traffic inspector for the Orange County highway department and was making a routine survey on Myford Road. He tried to make a radio call but found that the set wasn't working right. Seconds later the UFO appeared. Heflin thought that it was a plane, but quickly realized that it wasn't.

The UFO hovered briefly near the front of the truck and Heflin grabbed his camera. He took the first picture through the windshield before the UFO drifted across the road and headed to the northwest. Heflin took the second picture through the right window. The UFO continued to the northwest and he shot the third and final picture.

During the sighting, Heflin noticed several things about the craft. It seemed to be spinning. For a moment it seemed to lose its stability, the top tipped toward Heflin but seconds later it increased its speed. It gained altitude rapidly leaving a smoke ring behind. Heflin took a fourth picture of the smoke.

Back at the office Heflin was reluctant to mention the UFO and the pictures, but did show them to a few close friends. One of the friends convinced Heflin that he should try to sell the pictures to a magazine. According to the story the snapshots were returned by the publication because they were too controversial.

In the meantime friends asked for copies of the pictures and Heflin had several prints made. Then friends of friends got copies until nearly everyone in Santa Ana, California, had a set of photos. The local newspaper finally heard about the sighting, interviewed Heflin and made several additional copies of the pictures. There was some discussion of a lie detector test but Heflin wanted the newspaper to pay the costs and they refused.

After the newspaper account of the sighting, Heflin began to receive phone calls from all over the country. Dozens of people wanted copies of the

116

pictures, wanted to hear the story or to tell him what he had really seen. One of the callers said that he was a colonel in the North American Air Defense Command (NORAD) and told Heflin not to discuss the case before he had a chance to talk to him. The colonel never called back.

Marine officers had obtained the original photographs from Heflin and near the end of September, returned them, requesting a receipt. A few hours later, Heflin was visited by two "men from NORAD." They asked for and received the originals. That was the last time that the photos or the colonel from NORAD were seen.

In fairness to the Air Force, it should be pointed out that the man from NORAD was not. NORAD would not have dispatched the investigators for any UFO case. Most of the field work was done by an officer from the closest air force base. The Air Force didn't take evidence from witnesses as a rule and when they did borrow the evidence, they made a point of returning it. They were having enough trouble without being accused of stealing pictures. There probably were men who said that they were from NORAD, but they were lying.

Analysis of the photographs was done by various civilian and military agencies. All were impressed with the pictures, except the Air Force, and later, the Condon Committee. The Air Force claimed that it had made measurements showing that the object in the pictures was a small model. No one else, as that time, found any discrepancies in the photographs. Some went so far as to give unqualified support to the claims of authenticity.

Subsequent investigation, however, showed that the Air Force was correct. Computer enhancement techniques, developed after the end of Project Bluebook, showed a thin, black line above the UFO in both the pictures that are in sharp focus. This is probably a thread, supporting a small, man made model. Other measurements reveal the object to measure only inches in diameter.

The most interesting aspect of the case may be the reaction of the public to the Air Force investigation. Nearly everyone wanted to believe that the pictures were real. When the Air Force released its negative report, more than one UFO investigator claimed that the Air Force was hiding something. Now it seems that independent groups, with no ax to grind, are supporting the Air Force findings. More than twenty years after the fact, the consensus is, that the Heflin pictures are hoaxes.

117

After the UFO sightings peaked in 1966, about a year after Heflin, the Congress, along with certain segments of the public demanded that a real investigation be made. The Air Force chose the University of Colorado to make the study. In the end, the Condon Committee recommended that the Air Force stop wasting time and effort investigating something that didn't exist. The Air Force had reached similar conclusions earlier, but felt that the public wouldn't accept their findings without some sort of civilian research first.

In December, 1969, the Air Force closed Project Bluebook saying that there had been no evidence that UFO's posed a threat to the national security. With that, official investigations ended.

The cry of whitewash began before the ink was even dry on the Condon Report, and the Air Force press statements. UFO believers pointed to the 701 sightings in the Air Force files that were labeled as "unidentified." They claimed that others had, indeed, been labeled, but that the findings weren't accurate. And some claimed that for every one sighting the Air Force received, there were ten that went unreported.

But the public, in its fervor to believe, overlooked an important question. What was a significant number of unexplained sightings? If the Air Force couldn't explain 701 sightings, was that enough to suggest that there was something more to the UFO phenomena? Was there something that the Air Force, in its haste to explain and label, overlooked? Or, could it be, because there were so many people who wanted to believe, they would believe, no matter what the evidence showed, so that 701 sightings became a battle cry to them? Maybe if 701 couldn't be explained, then the Air Force wasn't trying hard enough. The aliens were out there.

But belief doesn't make it so. To prove that UFO's exist more than a desire to believe is needed. At least to the thinking person. But that didn't stop large numbers of people from listening to any one of a variety of sources that claimed to have superior knowledge of the aliens.

The first of these groups to attract large crowds of believers and followers was the contactees. Most claimed that they had been singled out by the UFO occupants, usually blond and female, to bring messages of peace and brotherhood back to the Earth. They "preached" what they had been told by the benevolent space brethren, wrote books with their words of wisdom and tried to convince "non-believers" with silver tongued arguments. Their supporters would not allow anything derogatory to be said about the contactees, and there was no reasoning with them. They had the answers and weren't interested in the facts, no matter how impressive the credentials of the detractor. And the contactees never offered any proof of their claims. They didn't have to because their followers accepted every word as the truth. The real question was, how many of the contactee reports made up a part of the 701?

Very little is heard about the contactees today. Maybe it is because we, as a group, have grown up, or maybe it is because our own travels into space have shown the contactees to be wrong. They still attract some followers, but the numbers are so small that it no longer pays. The contactees have, for the most part, moved into other fields and are not interested in UFO's. But the stigma of their activities has remained and there are still thousands who believe in them.

Many of the UFO researchers have condemned the followers of the contactees because they accepted the word of the contactee on faith. The researchers would know better than to fall into such a trap and they have avoided it, at least, when dealing with contactees. However, when it comes to the so-called "reliable" witness, they have accepted a great deal on faith. Because the witness is college educated, or a highly trained professional, the researcher has believed that the witness is reporting everything factually or accurately. The researcher has taken the easy way out and not pushed hard enough for the solution to the sighting.

For some, a police officer who makes a UFO report is to be believed. He is a trained observer, he is supposed to be truthful and not supposed to make mistakes. When he sees a UFO, it is just that, an unidentified flying object and "no amount of investigation will uncover a logical answer." Many accept such a report on faith with little or no further investigation. They know that they will never find an answer so why bother to look for one.

It is true that police officers are trained observers and most will write down what happened as they see it so that they don't have to rely on memory, but they are not astronomers or pilots, and do not regularly observe the sky. They can be fooled by a strange light or object in the night sky as easily as anyone else. When a police officer makes a UFO report, he probably is reporting something that he has seen, but it is up to the investigator to try to find an explanation for the case. It can't be left as unidentified just because it was made by a police officer.

Pilots fall in a similar category. They are highly trained technicians and are familiar with the sky. But, their reports can't be accepted without any investigation. They, too, can make mistakes. An Air Force crew once chased a light in the sky, at first believing it to be some kind of orange UFO. Moments later, they decided that it was a forest fire on the far horizon, but quickly realized that it was the moon, close to the horizon and seen through a thick layer of haze and dust. This is often the case of trained observers looking at something familiar and not being able to immediately identify it. All UFO sightings must be investigated before they can be accepted as something out of the ordinary.

Most serious investigators and researchers are aware of these problems but there is a large number of people who hold "field investigator" or "area investigator" or "regional investigator" status and who overlook some of these fundamental points. Hundreds of others see themselves as investigators and claim the title but will not accept the facts when presented. They will believe any story told by a UFO witness. And the problem is not only with investigators but with witnesses as well.

Not too long ago, a woman living in Utah had what she thought was an extraordinary experience. While driving home she saw a huge, softly glowing UFO near the road. It seemed to follow her for a few minutes and when she stopped, the UFO stopped, hovering above her. She watched as it slowly ascended. Finally, the glow dimmed and the UFO winked out of sight.

The woman was very excited about the sighting. She has always wanted to see a UFO and regretted that she didn't have her camera. Her daughter was with her and each of the women made a report of her observations. They knew it wasn't the moon or Venus because it had been so huge. The other stars were visible in the clear night sky and there was little wind. She had no explanation.

The following night, after she had made her report, an investigator followed her to the location of the sighting. Near a high school and behind some trees, they could see a glow similar to that of the UFO. The woman stayed in the car, but the investigator walked to the trees. He found a group of high school kids about to launch a hot air balloon filled with small candles. They had been there the night before and had launched the balloon then. The investigator was sure that it was just such a balloon that the woman and her daughter had seen.

Back at the car, he told her about the boys and the balloons. She would not believe him. She had seen a huge UFO and not a balloon. Although the balloons launched by the boys looked like what she had seen, she was sure that it did not explain her sighting. She wanted to see a UFO so badly that she would not accept the plain facts when they were set in front of her. Her sighting could easily be one of the Air Force's 701 unsolved sightings.

She no longer had a UFO sighting, but a belief that she had seen something strange. To believe, she needed to forget the facts and accept her observations based on her faith in the existence of UFO's.

The witnesses of a UFO event aren't the only ones who fail to recognize the facts and many UFO researchers, as well as buffs, have made that mistake. They have been presented with an overwhelming amount of evidence suggesting that the UFO experience being described didn't take place but they ignore the evidence and believe the tale.

In 1975, a large group of people, including many investigators, were invited to participate in a question and answer session involving a man who said that he had been taken into a UFO. A lie detector test had been arranged with a police officer who had graduated from one of the top polygraph schools, and had over twenty-five years experience. The two men were introduced to the group and each provided an opportunity to tell his story.

The UFO witness said that in November, 1953, while working for the railroad, he had seen a UFO. He had been driving on country roads and was going up an incline to a railroad crossing when the engine of the truck died. He pulled on the brake and tried to start the engine but failed. He then saw a bright light on the other side of the tracks and jumped from the truck before losing consciousness.

Sometime later he woke up apparently strapped to some kind of table. Near him, he could see a "mirror" that seemed to show the organs of his body. He could see his heart beating, his lungs expanding and contracting and even some movements along his brain. (Yes, I too recognize the scene. It's from a third rate science fiction film called "Killers From Space.")

Standing near him was a tiny creature that had a small chest and was covered with a greenish and rough skin. He could see no features on the face but did notice two holes on the side of the head. There was a strip of stiff hair on the top of the head, reminding the witness of the Indians in eastern New York (Mohawks). The creature's hands only had three digits, a thick thumb and two fingers. The interior of the room was brightly lighted and the light seemed to wash out the colors and details. His head was fastened to the table and all he could do was move his eyes.

After twenty minutes, he lost consciousness again and woke up next to his truck. The light was gone so he climbed into the cab. The engine started quickly and he drove back to the rail yard. A few minutes later, he returned to the site with friends, but they saw nothing.

The police sergeant was next. He explained, briefly, how the lie detector test was run earlier and that they had made three tests. Each test was made of ten questions but only three of the questions related to the UFO experience. There was, of course, a control question, so that the sergeant would be able to gauge the reactions of the subject.

Slowly, the police sergeant read the questions and reported his findings. "The third question was about seeing the UFO. I got a reaction. There was a reaction to the seventh question and there was a reaction when I asked if he believed the experience. There were reactions on all the relevant questions."

The third exam, made after the sergeant had talked to the witness for more than an hour ended the same way. "There were reactions on all the relevant questions, ranging from small up to high." The witness had not passed any of the tests.

The sergeant concluded, "He (the UFO witness) had not convinced himself that this incident had occurred. He said that he had not told many people because he thought no one would believe him." The sergeant looked at the other man and added, "I told him that I would report exactly what I found and he agreed. I had to conclude that this was a deception."

After the two reports were made, questions were asked. Most were directed at the UFO witness, in an attempt to gain more information about his sighting. For over an hour, fifteen people, each with a tape recorder, closely questioned the man. They wanted to know everything that he could tell. The police sergeant was virtually ignored.

One or two of the people did ask the sergeant a few questions but they were trying to find out if there could have been a mistake in his results. He explained that lie detectors have an accuracy approaching 95 percent and he had to say that he had no reason to believe the test was inaccurate. After a few more half-hearted attempts to break the lie detector test, the questioning reverted to the witness.

Fortunately, there was another test to be run. No one had to rely on only the police sergeant's interpretation of the lie detector test. A hypnotic regression session was arranged but participation was limited to only a few people. The report was made available to all who were interested.

After an exhausting two hour session, the hypnotist, who had been involved in dozens of UFO investigations, had an answer. Like the police sergeant, he worded his statement carefully so that he would not offend the witness. "He may have had an experience at one time, but it is now so buried in dreams, projections and sublimations that we might never get to the real experience, if there was one. There is no way that we could get to the facts."

Now, from two objective sources, the same answer surfaced. The UFO witness was a nice man, who .seemed to be sincere but who had probably not been on a flying saucer. Both the police sergeant and the hypnotist made it clear that they did not believe that the witness was consciously lying but that there was some doubt about the story. The witness may have had a vivid dream in 1953 and convinced himself that it may have happened. His subconscious was aware of the "real" nature of the experience and that was why there were the negative reactions.

The real problem is the fifteen people who were questioning the witness. They believed everything that he said, in spite of the results of the two tests. They were willing to believe that a lie detector will work on everything but a UFO report. The UFO witness had to be telling the truth because they wanted him to be telling the truth. They didn't want to be confused by mere facts.

The religious zeal of the fifteen people had shown through and they accepted, on faith, everything that the witness had said. When proof was offered that the sighting may not be any good, they ignored it. When additional evidence was later offered, they ignored that too.

The problem develops when these people begin to report on the experience to their various UFO organizations and groups. Since they believed it to be true, they report it as true. They overlook the evidence and eventually the case reaches a researcher interested in proving UFO's are extraterrestrial. It is added to the block of material to support the belief that UFO's are spacecraft. Maybe another of the 701.

Like the aforementioned case, today there is a large body of UFO information that is reported and repeated but that has very little basis in fact. Few are worried about that. As long as they can quote lists of cases, they can "prove" their point. When one case is shown to be defective, they can turn to a hundred or a thousand others. It makes no difference because they believe so firmly that they need no proof.

If they are pinned to the wall, having their best cases chopped out from under them, they can always resort to the theory that there are millions of "Earths" circling millions of "suns." Some of them must have life and that life must be more intelligent than the human race. There is no scientific proof of any of that, but there is a great deal of statistical evidence. However, it's a theory that the believers accept on faith.

So we see, suddenly, that maybe 701 sightings isn't a significant number. More than numbers is needed to prove that UFO's are spacecraft. It becomes apparent that the substances of the UFO phenomena is no more solid than the substance supporting the ancient astronauts.

It comes down to science and the scientific method. Should science, with its generalized conclusion that UFO's aren't real, be believed. What has science offered to suggest that they are right and the rest of us wrong?

It's interesting to note that in many UFO books, it is here that a certain statement appears. Science rejected the idea of rocks from the sky. In 1803, the French Academy of Science refused to believe that rocks could fall from the sky. Yet today we all know about meteors. Somehow this statement is meant to justify a rejection of modern science.

But, it can be taken too far. Almost no one tells you that science rejected the notion of rocks from the sky because the original idea showing it was a slipshod investigation, worthless of consideration. They also overlook the fact that a year later, in 1804, the French Academy of Sciences, those same scientists accepted the idea of rocks from the sky after they were presented with a carefully assembled package of "proof" that each of them could examine. They could independently test the results and duplicate them themselves.

We are told that the enlightened layman, without preconceived ideas stands a better chance of finding the "new" truth because he won't be hampered by all the things that he knows to be true, no matter how outdated his facts may be. Are these the same enlightened laymen who burned people for claiming that the Earth was not the center of the universe and who refused to look through Galileo's telescope because it was the work of the devil?

It all boils down to proof. It just isn't there. The Condon Report said that we could expect one visit every ten thousand years. Carl Sagan thinks that we have been visited, but in the ancient past. He doesn't think the modern UFO sightings are very impressive. I have to agree. To a point. And that is the basis for a new theory.

SOLUTIONS AND THEORIES

Nearly everyone has what he calls the answer to the UFO question. He may claim that they are extraterrestrial spacecraft, illusions, psychic phenomena, electrified plasma, swamp gas, birds, or hoaxes. The Air Force and the Condon Committee claimed that all but a very small number of sightings could be placed in a giant category labeled "misinterpretation of natural phenomena." Everyone agrees that 90 percent or 95 percent of all UFO sightings fit there. It is the small number that can't be explained in those terms that has everyone worried.

It could be that nearly everyone is looking for one answer that will mop up the remaining sightings. The believers in hardware UFO's, that is, extraterrestrial spacecraft, think that spaceships are the answer. The believers in ESP think that some sort of psychic phenomena is the answer. The enlightened might make a case for all the answers, at least, to some extent.

As a premise, we must assume that the Air Force was correct in their evaluation of the UFO phenomena. That is, most sightings can be attributed to simple mistakes. The Air Force was often ridiculed for claiming a sighting had a rational explanation when the rest of the UFO community assured us that the case was a bona fide UFO. The Heflin case is the, best example. In the 1960's and the 1970's, no one believed the Air Force answer of hoax. It was obvious that the Air Force was covering up. In the 1980's, with the improvement in computer enhancement techniques, we find the Air Force was right. The string supporting the "UFO" has been detected. The civilian researchers now agree with the Air Force. The Heflin case is a hoax.

It must also be assumed that the Air Force wouldn't have labeled a case unless they were sure that the label would hold up under scrutiny. It didn't mean that the public had to buy it, only that they honestly believed that they had the answer. Again, the Heflin case shows us that the Air Force did that.

The point of contention comes when glancing through the Air Force files, something I had the opportunity to do in 1975. While most people can accept that someone seeing a meteor under unusual circumstances might think they are seeing something other worldly, it is hard to believe that people could mistake the moon for a flying saucer. In the Air Force files, there is more than one case labeled as the "MOON."

Like nearly everyone else, I found that amusing. One multiple witness case studied by both civilians and military personnel was solved by the moon. On lectures I would explain that the Air Force had tried to fit anything into the sighting so that they could solve it. I recounted the joint military, civilian observation of the moon. It always got a big laugh.

In November, 1975, I stopped laughing. Grant County, Wisconsin, was the site of a miniature wave of UFO sightings. It involved everything that the researcher could want: Physical evidence, photos taken by a police officer, landings, cattle mutilations, electro-magnetic effects, multiple witnesses. And I was close enough to get there before the film was developed and the UFO's were gone.

The first disappointment was the pictures. What showed up on the film was not the object that the officer had tried to photograph. Each image looked like the other. And, no matter how the officer had held the camera, upright or tilted, the image was in the same place on the negative. The UFO was obviously an internal reflection.

The electromagnetic effects also vanished. Residents claimed that on the night the UFO's arrived, their television pictures had been blurry and erratic. Unfortunately, the same was true over most of Iowa and parts of Illinois. The problem wasn't UFO's, but transmission trouble from Chicago.

Then the landing disappeared, along with the physical evidence. The report stated that a TV antenna had been knocked down by a low flying UFO. Research showed there was no low flying UFO and instead a high wind had toppled the antenna.

And then, one of the officers suggested that they all had been seeing Jupiter, which was extremely bright. He pointed it out and sure enough, the descriptions of the high flying UFO fit with Jupiter.

The sheriff had an answer for the cattle mutilation. He thought the farmer had done it for the insurance money. The farmer lost an investment if the cow had died of natural causes. A local vet confirmed the cause of death. And the single mutilation didn't fit the pattern that was developing in other parts of the country.

The whole wave blew up under research, although one self styled UFO investigator had claimed it as an amazing sequence of events. But then came the topper. While I was at the police station, a call came in from a frightened man. He said that a brilliant disc shaped craft was hovering over his house and that the police should do something. An officer asked if I wanted a ride and I agreed. At the man's house, he dragged us into the backyard and pointed to the partly cloudy sky, screaming, "There. You see it. It's there."

And sure enough. There it was. The moon. Just as big and bright as it had always been. Momentarily I was stunned. I couldn't believe that an intelligent adult could get so caught up in a UFO wave that he couldn't recognize the moon. But that was exactly what happened. I was there. I saw it.

Other explanations in the Air Force files became less humorous. Venus, a culprit to the extreme, was blamed for hundreds of sightings. Easier to mistake for a UFO than the moon, but a real answer nonetheless.

Again, I was in the Cedar Rapids, Iowa, Civil Defense Center when a call came in from a woman who was watching something in the western sky. It was extremely bright and darting around in a small circle. The Civil Air Patrol squadron commander dismissed the sighting as a weather balloon without going out to look. In reality, it was Venus. I saw it.

Former President Jimmy Carter fell into the same trap. He reported seeing an extremely bright light in the western sky that was darting around. Venus. The times and the directions given by Carter fit with the astronomical tables.

The problem is that most people don't know that the eye is constantly moving. When staring at a large area, these tiny adjustments aren't noticed, but when the object is a point of light, it will seem to jump around. The cause is the eye and not the motion of the object. Next time you are outside, pick out a bright star, Sirius for example, and stare at it. See if it doesn't seem to jump around. That aberration of sight might solve a few of the unidentified cases being carried by the Air Force. Maybe only ten or twenty, but it would reduce the number that many think is so important.

The longer researchers explore the Air Force files, the more they find to support the belief that dozens of UFO sightings were solved. The Air Force searched long and hard to find answers. There was a belief that they searched too long and too hard, and then began making up the solutions when they couldn't find one that fit. An overzealous officer at any air base might have fallen into that trap, but as a whole, such a conspiracy of silence isn't in evidence.

Another problem that the Air Force may have had was the expanding technology. Many of the early cases are based on radar sightings. In many of the instances, there was no corresponding visual sighting. The suggestion is that the radar was picking up something that it wasn't supposed to pick up and perhaps the quality of the equipment was better than either the Air Force or the operator were aware.

A case in point was the time that we almost went to war because the newly operational radars of the Air Defense Command picked up what looked like hundreds of missiles streaking over the North pole. A quick check showed that the moon was reflecting the radar signal. No one expected the radar to be that good.

The point is, the Air Force was right more often than not. All they left unsolved were a tiny number of the overall reports. And it may have been that they couldn't solve those because they didn't have the scientific knowledge that is just now coming our way. We can always refer to the Heflin case. Had there been computer enhancement techniques in 1965, the pictures might have died then, rather than now.

In 1967, Philip Klass purposed a theory that some of the UFO's might be balls of plasma. It was his belief that ionized air, under the right conditions, could begin to glow and take on a saucer shape. Klass went a little further, explaining that many of the UFO sightings near electrical power lines, might be the result of the ionization of the air. The UFO community scoffed at the idea.

It is doubtful that Klass ever intended to explain all the unidentified reports in the Air Force files. It might, however, explain a small number of them, and UFO research is supposed to be a search for other answers. It must be granted that Klass's theory did explain a number of sightings. And again, the number of unidentified shrinks.

Klass's theory was good as far as it went, but now there is information of a related phenomena, and that phenomena might explain even more of the

128

unidentifieds. ABC Television's 20/20 presented the first in depth analysis of the theory.

According to them, Doctor Michael Persinger, after studying about six thousand UFO sightings, believed that some of the mysterious objects were "earthquake lights." Japanese scientists provided Persinger with a photo of earthquake lightning thereby assisting in the redefinition of the theory.

Further refinement came when Doctor Brian Brady of the U.S. Bureau of Mines in Denver, Colorado was contacted.

ABC's 20/20 brought the two men together in Denver, and ran a series of experiments. Brady, using cylinders of quartz bearing rock, compressed them in a machine until they shattered. His instruments registered discharges of energy just prior to the shattering of the rock. ABC, using a special camera, made motion pictures of the luminous displays as the cylinders shattered. The film slowed the motion of the lights until it could be seen that they were not streaks of light, but glowing balls of energy that were growing in the electrically charged air. Brady estimated that the displays would last for only a fraction of a second because of the size of the samples used. If a survey was made of an earthquake fault that ran for miles, the stresses of the shifting Earth's surface might cause displays that lasted for long periods of time and create balls of energy that were huge.

Persinger was able to take the theory further yet. He said that the natural shape of the luminous display would be spherical, unless the balls were spinning and he believed that the natural tendency would be for them to spin. Then the form would degenerate into a saucer shape with a slight dome on top and bottom and the whole thing would glow. He was describing the classic UFO.

Such a theory was fine, although it did nothing to explain reports of UFO occupants. Using the Travis Walton abduction as their base, 20/20 explained the claim that Walton was taken into a UFO.

According to research, the area where Walton was working that evening was seismically active. The ground contains the quartz bearing rock that is needed to produce the electrical discharges. Walton, and his co-workers, described the UFO as measuring twenty to twenty-five feet in diameter and about eight feet thick. They were coming through the trees when they first spotted the glow.

Walton told investigators that he then approached the thing. He could hear a sound, and that the UFO was wobbling. Walton said that he decided that it was time to go and stood up to run. When he did, a beam of light shot from the UFO, striking him in the head and chest. Five days later, he awoke, remembered almost nothing of the last five days, and called home. He told researchers that he could remember two hours when he was on board the flying saucer and nothing else.

Persinger seemed to think that this would be the classic example of his luminous displays. If an object, or a person, approached near enough, that could change the magnetic field enough to cause part of the ball to become unstable. The result would be a discharge of electricity, not unlike lightning, that would strike the object that had moved into the area. Persinger stressed that only part of the ball would be unstable. The rest of it would continue to glow and pulsate. Persinger then went on to explain that an electrical charge to the brain could alter the brain's activity and cause hallucinations. He also said that such a jolt could induce amnesia. A person suffering from that form of amnesia would be able to survive in society, would be able to cope with the world and would appear normal, but would remember 'nothing. Finally he would wake up and find himself in an unknown place. He would have no memory of how he got there. A precise description of the Walton case.

The Persinger/Brady theory seems to explain another segment of the UFO phenomena. It finally comes down to this. With our scientific knowledge expanding as fast as it is, we are explaining more and more of the unidentified sightings. The earthquake lights, and the energy from the shifting of the Earth's crust make good sense now. It tends to explain a number of the sightings.

There is one point that the 20/20 story did not make. Before the UFO experience, Travis Walton was interested in the phenomena. He read books on the subject and discussed it with friends. He had expressed a desire to see a real flying saucer and had said that he wouldn't hesitate to approach one if he had the chance. This is not an indictment of Walton. There are thousands who fit the description. But the point is important.

Walton, before he was hit with the beam of light, believed that he was seeing a spacecraft. He had read enough to know what the crews were supposed to look like. The Hill case had been well publicised. The Hickson-Parker affair had been national news the day after it happened years earlier. In short, Walton was believer.

One psychologist said that he could see where a traumatic experience like the one that 20/ 20 suggested, could induce a specific hallucination.

Walton's last conscious thought would have been about alien creatures. The electrical discharge that hit him could destroy his memory of the next few days, and yet, leave the hallucination intact. In other words, the intervention of alien creatures is no longer needed to explain the sighting made by Walton.

The new evidence then, suggests still another way for UFO's to be generated by nature. It fits with the general conclusion that there is no one theory that explains all the unidentified sightings. There are many. Each chips away at the foundation of thousands of sightings, until there are none left. Each unidentified sighting topples. It was a hoax, it was Venus, it was the moon, or ball lightning, or plasma, or earthquake lights. Whatever.

We are left with the ashes of a belief in the extraterrestrial because the visitors are no longer needed to explain the UFO phenomena. The Air Force was right. Philip Klass was right. The Condon Committee was right. Believers can only voice the one conclusion of the Condon Committee that all UFO believers hold dear. The reports said that we could expect one extraterrestrial visit every ten thousand years. What they didn't tell us was when we could start counting the years.

Did the ten thousand years start when the human race first invented civilization? Or when the Egyptians refined it? Or at the time of Christ?

Or did it begin when the first ancestors of the human race walked the Earth? According to some theories, our first relatives are about three million years old. That would mean that there are the possibilities for over three hundred visits by the extraterrestrials.

Or, can we refine that? Begin counting, say, with the Neanderthal, about one hundred thousand years ago? That means ten visits. Or possibly begin with Homo sapiens? Down to three or four visits.

I'll opt for the four visits. And I'll opt for the majority of them coming at least ten thousand years ago. In other words, the last visit came prior to the Egyptians. It came about the time the first societies in the Middle East were forming. Small bands of men and women who were beginning to learn the techniques of agricultural and living in groups and working together for survival.

But that leaves me with one visit unaccounted for. One. And it leads right into the middle of the October Scenario.

131

THE OCTOBER SCENARIO

One visit every ten thousand years, Condon and the others have said. One chance every ten thousand years to make physical, face to face to contact with aliens from another planet. Just one chance.

Then we hit October, 1973 a time of unprecedented UFO activity. Different from the other waves. A timepsan that might be a prelude to other visits, especially after all the information that was taken in the Hickson-Parker, Roach, Ramstead, Proctor and Llanca abductions, and gathered by all the UFO landings. After the aliens draw their conclusions, write their papers (if they write papers) and make their computer analysis, (if they make computer analysis), there will probably be more UFO sightings.

But why then? Why claim October 1973 as our one visit, and not the fall of 1967, or the summer of 1952, or the summer of 1947, during the other great "UFO waves?" Obviously because the evidence points to October 1973. That was why I made the studies of the other eras. That is why I examined the ancient astronauts. That is why I argued for significant numbers. And until October of 1973, they just weren't there. Before October of 1973, the whole UFO phenomena made almost no sense whatsoever. And that was because we were misinterpreting natural phenomena.

In the beginning of this book, I made the statement that the UFO sightings

133

in the fall of 1973 differed from all the other waves because of the number of occupant reports. The reason, I believe, is that the creatures on the flying saucers had their one chance to collect their data and they went after it with a vengence during October of 1973.

Another brief look at the sightings prior to 1973 shows this. Almost every one of the sightings could be explained. Those sightings that couldn't, showed no pattern, other than being single witness. The great photographic cases tended to fall, one by one, as new techniques for analyzing photos were developed. We were left with very little hard data and left with no discernable patterns. Until 1973.

A second point. After the 1973 wave of sightings, the incident of reports of UFO occupants dropped off again. More high flying discs, but not many reports of landings. More noise to confuse and confound. There are other things. The occupants reported in 1973 were described in similar ways. For the most part they were short, very human looking, as opposed to humanoid (meaning two arms and two legs and a single head). Their ships were all described in similar terms. There was very little variation, and the variations could be attributed to the differences of the witnesses.

Police officers are familiar with the problems when dealing with multiple eyewitnesses. Seven people see the same thing, and seven people describe the event differently. Small variations in the descriptions are to be eliminated as noise. They don't fit the pattern and therefore don't belong in the sighting files. Another question may be, "Why do I accept the Air Force conclusions and the Condon study after they have been ridiculed by nearly everyone who studies UFO's? The answer is that I don't believe they have deserved the ridicule they have gotten. Look again at the Heflin case. Everyone said that the pictures were good, maybe the best ever. Every study suggested that they were real, except for the Air Force. Now it turns out the Air Force was right. The pictures were faked.

But the Condon and the Air Force quit studying UFO's in 1969. They stopped looking four years too soon. All the criterian that they longed to find, appeared during the flap of 1973. And they had said that UFO's didn't exist.

Another important question is probably, "When will they return?" That is very hard to answer because we don't know where they came from, how long it took them to get here, and whether or not we made a favorable impression on them. Maybe their study is completed and this specific group will not be back. It doesn't mean that there aren't other groups out there who may eventually reach the Earth.

So, it all boils down to an answer that many will not find acceptable. UFO sightings prior to October 1973 are the result of a wide variety of natural and man-made phenomena. For all the debate, photos and supposed physical evidence, there were no alien spacecraft in our skies. Sightings after October 1973 fall into the same category. There were hoaxes and fakes and misidentifications, but no spacecraft.

But during October 1973 (and a few weeks prior to and following it) there were extraterrestrial spacecraft visiting Earth. There were aliens walking our planet. There were encounters between the human race and the creatures from another star system.

This is the only time in recorded history that it happened. The evidence in October 1973 is so different from the evidence of the other waves, that no other conclusion is possible. We had our one chance. This was it, the October Scenario.

Unfortunately, these weren't the types of contact that have been envisioned by science fiction writers and movie makers, but is almost a carbon copy of the way we would act in a similar circumstance, providing we don't recognize the locals as possessing a superior intelligence. Our moon landings illustrate the point. For a few days, two men tramped all over the moon, digging up all the samples they could carry, and performing all the experiments that they could cram into the short time they had. When they were gone, the "UFO" they were using went with them.

The analogy breaks down because of the relative closeness of the moon to the Earth. It allowed for multiple moon landings. But these came over a period of a couple of years. Since then, there have been no "UFO's" on the moon.

Now, expand the magnitude of the adventure. Say that they have to travel thirty light years to get here. Because of the distances, they could dispatch only one crew to this portion of the galaxy. Since the last visit was ten thousand years ago, their data shows that there isn't much on Earth, but still the ship goes out. One ship, on a scale say, of the Starship Enterprise from STAR TREK. Lots of people to do research, and a couple of shuttles to ferry them around.

They find the Earth teeming with life. Civilization has exploded all over the face of the planet. But they have only one or two months, to make their survey. They gather as much data as they can in the month they have. And during this one visit the aliens make sure that they gather the genetic material to continue their research.

Plant and animals tissues are fine. So are rocks. But the real key to the study of Earth is the intelligent life.

They know that a human cannot reproduce with an individual from their society, but maybe their preliminary studies had shown that there are laws of genetics just as there are laws of physics. They may have learned that these laws of genetics are universal. Given that they have had a chance to test their laws on other worlds and therefore understand.certain biological applications, they would have the knowledge that could be applied to growing biological samples from our genetic material.

This explains the extended contact the aliens had with people of Earth. It explains why they were questioning the abductees so closely. The biological necessities had been covered by their studies on their home world and the other worlds they had visited. The psychological studies of the human mind could only be made on this planet. Those theories and studies had to be built from scratch. Once the genetic material was gathered, a relatively short process, they needed to study the psychological aspects. That was why the people had to be taken on board the craft.

Although Pat Roach and Susan Ramstead hinted at this. Hinted at the production of humans, it was Leigh Proctor that provided the final clue. She was told that she would want to see the baby. The implication is that there would be a baby and although it might not be the combination of the egg and sperm as is done on this planet but a full clone, it would be a human baby. It might have been a test for Leigh too. The aliens wanted to see her reaction to the idea that she had supplied the genetic material for a baby.

Then, when their time is up, (and their studies completed, or not as the case may be) they blast back into space, taking all their "UFO's" with them. When they are gone, the last sighting is made and things on Earth return to normal. No more flying saucers from other planets. Just more misinterpretations of natural phenomena.

So the October Scenario is the theory that October 1973 was the only period of real UFO sightings. The aliens were gathering samples for study on their return to their home world. They used their time on the Earth to gather data and to take genetic samples to produce their own human subjects. After all the genetic material is easier to transport than full grown samples who might cause other problems once the trip has begun.

We are left only with the hope that they will have found us interesting. That now they know the address, they will be back. That the people who shot at them, the people who fled from them didn't make the major impression. It comes down to this. We had our visit in October 1973. The October Scenario. Because of the noise, that is, the false UFO sightings that had bombarded us for the three decades prior to that, we didn't recognize the sightings for what they were. We can only hope that if the opportunity arises again, we will be smart enough to see it. That we will make the most of it. Because. It doesn't happen that often.

Part IV

The Alternative View

ANTONIO VILLAS-BOAS

When the story of Barney and Betty Hill's abduction broke in 1961, there were very few who believed them. Most UFO researchers were content to chase the lights in the sky. They tended to laugh at any reports of a landing or occupants. George Adamski had ruined that field with his tales of beautiful Venusians and trips to other worlds.

The Hill story varied from those enough so that serious researchers, at least, listened. Neither Barney nor Betty remembered anything consciously, and because the story evolved from the visits they were making to a Boston psychiatrist, researchers continued to listen.

But that acceptance was very slow. Even today the debate continues, with both sides, skeptics and believers, able to use scientific evidence to support their positions. Imagine how a young South American farmer felt in October, 1957, when he stepped forward with a story of abduction. Not only did he see the craft, but he was confused by a naked woman who had an obvious interest in him.

Antonio Villas-Boas told his story to outsiders the first time in February, 1958. Barney and Betty Hill wouldn't have their experience for another three years and it would be another couple of years before it was reported by UFO researchers. Villas-Boas certainly couldn't have read about them, so their case provided no guidance and no incentive. His was the first of a kind.

According to him, "It all began on the night of October 5, 1957." Villas-Boas was in his room after a party and for some reason, he looked out to the horse corral. In the middle of it he could see a bright, fluorescent light. It seemed to sweep upward, into the sky, but there was no object over it. Joao, Villas-Boas' brother also saw the light. Neither of them had an explanation for it.

A few days later, Villas-Boas was working in a field when he saw another bright light. This one was about three hundred feet in the air, shaped like a wheel and was intensely bright. Villas-Boas called to another brother who didn't care to see it. For twenty minutes, Villas-Boas chased the light from one end of the field to the other but he finally grew tired. As he left the area, he glanced back to it several times and saw it throwing off rays like the setting sun. It finally just disappeared.

The next night, it came back for the second time. Villas-Boas was plowing the field late because it was too hot to work in the sunlight. At one in the morning, he noticed an extremely bright red star overhead. He watched it and realized that it was moving, growing larger as it approached. Villas-Boas hesitated, wondering what to do, and in those few seconds, the light changed into an egg-shaped craft descending toward his freshly plowed field. It stopped to hover over him, its light so bright that Villas-Boas could no longer see his own headlights.

For two minutes, the UFO hovered and Villas-Boas stared. He thought of driving away from it, but he knew it could easily catch the tractor. The ground was too soft for him to run very fast. The UFO moved again, diving toward the ground, and for the first time Villas-Boas could see the details on it.

The bright red light seemed to come from the front of the craft that looked like an elongated egg. There were purple lights near the large red one, and there was a small red light on a flattened cupola that spun rapidly. As the UFO approached the ground, three telescoping legs slid from under the machine.

The legs, like those of a camera tripod were for landing, and as Villas-Boas realized that, he turned the tractor and stepped on the accelerator, trying to escape. He made it only a few feet before the engine sputtered and died and the headlights went out. He tried to start it but the ignition didn't seem to work. When it failed to start, he opened the door on the side of the tractor opposite the UFO and jumped out. He had only taken a few steps when something touched his arm. Villas-Boas spun, looking at the short creature that had grabbed him. Struggling to escape, he put a hand on the creature's chest and pushed. The creature released him, staggered backward and then fell. As Villas-Boas turned to run, three other creatures grabbed him and lifted him froth the ground. He twisted, trying to jerk his arms free so that he could fight the aliens who held him tightly. He shouted for help and the sound of his voice seemed to fascinate the creatures, but they didn't relax their grips on him.

A door had opened in the craft and there was a narrow, metal ladder extending from it to the ground. The aliens tried to lift Villas-Boas into the machine but he grabbed the narrow railing on the ladder. One of the creatures peeled his hand from the flexible metal, and he was forced through the door.

The room was larger with a metal rod running from the floor to the ceiling and Villas-Boas thought that it held up the roof. To one side there was an oddly shaped table surrounded by backless chairs. For several minutes, Villas-Boas and the aliens stood in the room. The creatures talked among themselves in a series of low, growling sounds while they held Villas-Boas. Finally they began to strip his clothes from him carefully so that they didn't tear anything. When he was naked, one of the aliens began to "wash" him with an oily looking liquid that made him shiver as it dried.

As the aliens worked around him, Villas-Boas studied them. They wore a tight-fitting jump suit made of soft, unevenly stripped cloth. The cloth reached up their necks and over their heads almost like the hoods of wetsuits worn by skindivers. Villas-Boas had the impression that the hood was some kind of helmet because it hid everything except the alien's eyes.

There didn't seem to be any tanks for an air supply and Villas-Boas was unable to explain this. He did say that the helmets seemed to be almost twice as tall as the head. All of the aliens seemed to be shorter than Villas-Boas, only about five feet tall. He made a point of telling researchers that he was sure that he could have beaten any of them in a fair fight, but that five of them were too many for him. Three of the aliens moved Villas-Boas to another, small, square room. They entered through a swinging door that fit so snugly into the wall that he could not see where it had been. Two other aliens, carrying a large vessel with rubber hoses, approached. The hose was fastened to his chin, he felt a scratching and saw the clear, glass vessel fill with his blood. The procedure was repeated. When the hoses were removed, Villas-Boas felt a burning and itching on his chin. When the creatures finished, they gathered their equipment and they all left.

Villas-Boas inspected the room for a few minutes, seeing only a large couch in the middle of it. Since he was feeling tired, he went over to sit down and then noticed a strange smell in the air. From the walls, about head high, he noticed a gray smoke pouring into the room. Its thick, oily smell made him sick. For minutes he fought the feeling but it continued and he finally vomited.

Feeling better, Villas-Boas sat back on the couch, waiting. After thirty minutes, maybe longer, there was a noise at the door. He turned in time to see a woman entering, a naked woman. She came in slowly, watching Villas-Boas. She stepped unhurriedly to him and embraced him.

She was short, under five feet tall. She had light colored hair, almost white, as if it had been bleached heavily. She had blue eyes that were slanted to give her an Arabian look. Her face was wide with high cheekbones but her chin was very pointed, giving her whole face an angular look. She was slim, with high, very pointed breasts. Her stomach was flat and her thighs were large. Her hands looked normal and were small.

When the door closed again, the woman began to caress him, showing him exactly what she wanted. Given the circumstances, Villas-Boas was surprised that he could respond but he felt desire for her growing. She kept rubbing him, leading him and in moments they were on the couch, Villas-

144

Boas forgetting everything except her. Almost before he realized what was happening, they were joined and according to him, she responded as any woman would.

They stayed on the couch, petting, and in minutes both were ready again. Villas-Boas tried to kiss her but she refused, preferring to nibble his chin. When they finished a second time, she began to avoid him. As she stood up, the door opened and one of the alien men stepped in, calling to the woman. Before she left, she smiled at Villas-Boas, pointed to her stomach and then to the sky. It was then that he realized that she had flaming red pubic hair.

One of the men came back and handed Villas-Boas his clothes. While dressing, he noticed that his lighter was gone. He thought that it might have been lost during his escape attempt.

The alien directed him out of the small room and into another where the crew members were sitting, talking, or rather growling to themselves. He was left out of the discussion, the aliens ignoring him so he tried to fix the details in his mind. On a table, near the aliens was a square box with a glass lid, and a clock like face. There were markings corresponding to three, six and nine, and four marks at twelve. As he looked at it, the idea that he should take it, as proof of his adventure, gripped him. He edged his way closer and when none of the aliens were looking at it, Villas-Boas grabbed it. Before he could even take a closer look at it, one of the creatures jumped toward him and pushed him away.

At last another of the aliens mentioned for him to follow. None of the others even looked up as they walked to the entrance and the door. It was again open, with the ladder extending to the ground, but they didn't go down it. Instead, they stepped onto a platform that went around the ship. Slowly they walked along it as the alien pointed out various features. Since he didn't speak, Villas-Boas didn't know the purpose of any of the things he was shown. There were machines with purplish lights. He glanced at the cupola that emitted a greenish light and that was making a sound like a vacuum cleaner as it slowly spun.

When the tour was over, he was taken to the door. The alien pointed to the ladder and motioned Villas-Boas down it. At the bottom, he stopped and looked back, but the alien hadn't moved. Instead, he pointed to himself, then to the ground and finally toward the sky. He signalled Villas-Boas to step back as he disappeared into the UFO.

The ladder telescoped into itself as the door began to vanish. When it was closed, there was no seam or crack visible. The lights began to brighten as those on the cupola began to spin faster and faster until the ship lifted quietly into the sky. It stopped to hover about a hundred feet above the ground. The buzzing from it increased as it spun faster, until it was revolving at blurring speed. The colors flashed through the spectrum before settling on a bright, blinding red. As it changed color, it changed direction, causing a loud roar. It then shot to the south, disappearing in seconds.

Villas-Boas returned to his tractor and noticed it was nearly 5:30 a.m. He had been on the UFO for over four hours. He tried to start the engine but it still didn't work. He climbed down to look at the engine and discovered that the battery cables had been disconnected. When he hooked them up, the tractor started easily.

He was sure that the cables hadn't come loose by themselves and in fact, claimed that he checked them before he left the house. He said that he believed the aliens had done it so that he couldn't escape from them if he had been able to break their hold on him.

Villas-Boas didn't tell anyone, except his mother, about the sighting until February, 1958. Then, after reading several UFO stories in a Brazilian magazine, he contacted Joao Martins, who, with the help of APRO's Doctor Olavo Fontes, interviewed him. Both were impressed with Villas-Boas' sincerity. Martins told him that he didn't think the story would be published because it was so strange. Villas-Boas seemed disappointed so they suggested that he contact a newspaper. He declined.

The whole thing leaves us with one big question. Did Villas-Boas spend four hours on a spaceship crewed by creatures from another planet? His story suggests that he did. He wasn't sophisticated enough to invent a story

146

that avoids the pitfalls of a hoax. He didn't have the education or knowledge to know how to fool the investigators. Based on what he told them, and the way he told them, we almost have to conclude that it is the truth. But with a case like this, more evidence is needed. Something more needs to be added. And that may be the alternative to the October Scenario.

BARNEY AND BETTY HILL

The landmark case of the UFO abduction phenomena is the report submitted by Barney and Betty Hill. It is the case that became the standard by which all other such reports are judged. They set the tone for the future, and their case is the one that is usually mentioned first when the conversation turns to UFO's and abductions.

Like all the others, the Hills were caught in a lonely area, taken to a ship, examined and then released. Like many of the others, neither Betty nor Barney consciously remembered anything about the incident. There were a few dreams that brought the incident to mind, but it was only after hypnotic regression that all the details of the experience were recalled.

On September 19, 1961, the Hills were returning from a vacation. About 10 p.m. they stopped for coffee. Before they got back to the car, they figured that they would be home by 3 o'clock. As they drove along Highway 3, Betty Hill noticed a bright star near the moon. She was sure that it hadn't been there before, and she was sure that it was getting brighter. Finally, she pointed it out to Barney and he told her that it was probably a satellite.

Several times during the next hour, the Hills stopped. Once or twice they used a pair of binoculars to try to see detail behind the light. Betty was sure that she was seeing something out of the ordinary, but Barney kept insisting that it was nothing more unusual than a plane or a satellite.

The object remained to their right as they continued their trip. Betty thought that she could see a "flattened" disc through the binoculars. She also thought that it was dropping toward the ground in a very erratic pattern, losing some altitude, leveling for a few moments and then dropping again.

Finally, in the Indian Head section of the White Mountains, the object slipped to a position in front of the car, about eighty feet above the ground. Now the Hills could see the lighted edge of the UFO and a row of windows. Barney, realising that it was no airplane, stopped the car.

Betty handed Barney the binoculars and the UFO moved to the left side of the highway. He opened his door and stepped out to see better. Through the binoculars, he could see about seven figures watching him. There was a sudden burst of activity behind the windows as all the creatures but one turned away. Both Betty and Barney later described the creatures as having a cold precision, like German officers.

As Barney stared, he began to get the impression that the aliens were going to capture him. He felt drawn to the object. He now knew that the UFO wasn't anything conventional. Betty Hill said that her husband began to laugh, almost hysterically, and said, "They're going to capture us." He leaped into the car and they sped off. A few minutes later, Betty rolled down the window to see where the UFO was.

They hadn't gotten too far when they heard a series of beeping sounds. The car seemed to vibrate with each beep. Both of them began to feel drowsy. A while later, they heard the beeps again and noticed a sign that said Concord was seventeen miles away. They arrived home two hours later than they had planned.

During the next several days, the Hills discovered a series of things that they couldn't explain. Barney found a spot on his groin. Betty, for some reason, took the clothes that she had been wearing the night of the trip and hid them in the back of the closet. There were shiny spots on the trunk of the car. When they reached home, the trunk was unlocked, although Barney claimed he had locked it earlier.

For over a year, the Hills tried to forget the night they had driven home. But Barney began to exhibit several medical troubles. He had ulcers and high blood pressure. He went to a doctor and mentioned the UFO incident in passing. It wasn't until 1963 that the Hills went to Doctor Benjamin Simons who performed hypnotherapy on them.

150

Under hypnosis, both Betty and Barney began to relate the experiences they had after the first series of beeping sounds. They found themselves on a dirt road with some kind of roadblock at the end of it. Several creatures from the object surrounded their car and then led them to the disc-shaped UFO.

Separated by the aliens, the Hills were subjected to a variety of medical exams. Barney Hill said that he was put on an examining table that was too short for him. His legs hung over the end. They turned him over and looked at his back and finally turned him a second time. The creatures seemed fascinated by Barney's false teeth.

As the exam continued, a few more creatures entered the room. There was some rustling around and Barney felt something scratch his left arm. The aliens who had come in, left, and one of those remaining moved around his body.

When they finished, they put his shoes back on and got him off the table. He was escorted out of the ship and sent down a road. He could see the car sitting there. He walked to it and opened the door. Then he saw Betty walking down the road. She walked around the front of the car and got in the passenger's side. Betty Hill's experience on the craft didn't vary much from Barney's. Her accounts were more detailed, but that might be because, as she remembers, Barney kept his eyes closed during most of the abduction, so he didn't see as much.

Betty also "talked" with the creatures. They told her, for example, that Barney would be all right. He was in another room because they only had enough equipment in the one room to do one person at a time.

Betty reported that during her examination, the creatures touched her with a series of strange instruments. They took skin scrapings, pulled hair from her head, and took a fingernail clipping. But the most important aspect of the examination may be the needle that Betty claimed was pushed into her navel. Betty told the "leader" that it was painful and he passed a hand over her eyes. That stopped the pain-

Betty also provided a detailed description of the creatures. They were humanoid, only about five feet tall. They had large, slanting eyes, and small flattened noses. Their bodies seemed to be slightly out of proportion, They had large chests. They all seemed to be wearing shiny black uniforms and black hats with bills.

During the examination, Betty carried on a conversation with the creature

151

that she thought of as the leader. According to her, they didn't really speak, they "thought" at one another. Under hypnosis, Betty refused to describe the leader, a point that Doctor Simons thought was significant.

After the examination was over, Betty and the leader talked a few minutes more. Betty asked where they were from and the leader showed her a star map, which she later drew under hypnosis. According to the map, and a few researchers, it meant that the aliens were from Zeta 1 or Zeta 2 Reticuli, a double star about thirty-seven light years from Earth.

Betty was then escorted off the ship and joined Barney in the car. After a second series of beeps, both seemed to "awaken" far down the highway from where they had been.

The hypnotherapy took several months. When it was over, Simons said that he thought the Hills were recounting a fantasy. He believed that Betty had originated it and through telling Barney her dreams, had given it to him. Simons believed that because Barney's account was less detailed than Betty's.

Several UFO skeptics have noted other discrepancies in the Hill's story. Robert Sheaffer has said that when the Hills first spotted the UFO near the moon, they said they had seen a second star. In other words, near the moon on the night the Hills saw their saucer, Jupiter and Saturn were high in the sky. The Hill story makes no mention of Saturn, and Sheaffer believes that the original UFO might have been Saturn.

Because of the nature of the report, that is, an abduction by alien beings, the account, like all the others, is still wrapped in controversy. That controversy isn't going to be eliminated easily.

AN ALTERNATIVE
TO THE OCTOBER SCENARIO

Out of all the UFO sightings prior to 1973, why select the Villas-Boas and the Hill abductions as the only ones to be true? Obviously because they are the only reports that fit into the pattern established in 1973. Couple Villas-Boas to the 1957 wave since his abduction was in the middle of it, and the pattern is strengthened. Both of them, Hill and Villas-Boas, or either, or neither, might be true, and if they are, they can add a frightening note to the October Scenario.

The first thing that should be examined is the Villas-Boas case. Not only was it a "first" but it also provides a major clue about the Alternative to the October Scenario.

There are hundreds of things that can be said for the report. Villas-Boas didn't, for example, come forward until a series of pictures had been given widespread publicity in South America. Although he claims his sighting was made on October 15, some two weeks before the 1957 sightings in Levelland, Texas, and the desert southwest, his report was made three months after them. Certainly he could have heard of those sightings, the reports of two soldiers injured by a UFO over a Brazilian fort, and finally, he could have seen the pictures taken at Trindade Island in December, 1957.

It could be argued that the story was a sexual fantasy of Villas-Boas that had taken a turn into reality because of some psychological aberration. However, the story of the craft, the alien men and their descriptions take the dominant place in the report. The sexual aspects seemed to embarrass Villas-Boas and it was only with reluctance that he would mention them.

Another reason to suspect that it wasn't just a sexual fantasy is Villas-Boas' insistence that he could have taken any of the aliens singly, in a fair fight. He wanted his interviewers to understand that. It was almost as if he was ashamed of his poor performance during his capture, and was trying to explain how they had managed, with very little difficulty, to drag him to the ship. In a fantasy, or a hoax, the capture would have left several of the aliens dead or wounded before they overwhelmed him with superior numbers.

There were several areas where researchers interviewing Villas-Boas had questions. They wanted to know, for example, how the aliens breathed if their heads were covered with strange helmets with tubes sprouting from them, but no evidence of air tanks. Villas-Boas responded that he hadn't thought of that and that he didn't know. Each time he was confronted with questions of that nature, he said that he didn't know. In cases of hoax, the witness always has answers for such questions.

The other area that bothered researchers was the idea that Villas-Boas was being used for some kind of reproductive experiment. It was suggested that, for such an experiment to work, the aliens would have to provide the female subject since the pregnancy would occur only if she was ready.

The problem with that is that the female would almost have to be human for it to succeed. Everything we know about genetics says that it is impossible to cross-breed different species. It is possible for closely related animals to reproduce such as the lion and the tiger, the cow and the buffalo, or the jackal and the coyote, but it doesn't work if the biological division is too great. Cellular structure, chromosomes and DNA seem to get in the way. It would be extremely unlikely for an alien race to have a DNA molecule that would allow fertilization by a human. If they even have a DNA molecule. And all that overlooks the crude nature of the experiment. Using blood and tissue samples makes much more sense, and Villas-Boas said the aliens took both.

154

The answer that has been offered is that the aliens, attempting to gather sperm, were using the method they thought the least harmful to the human subject. That doesn't carry much weight when the cruel, calculating aliens of the Pat Roach abduction are remembered. They didn't care about her or her emotional state, as long as they gathered the information that they wanted.

Of course, Roach reported that she saw a human on board the UFO. He was working with the aliens, was taller than them, had five forgers to their three, and had graying hair. If that case was a factual report of reality, then it means that the woman Villas-Boas met could have been human. It would also explain why the aliens were wearing helmets that covered everything but their eyes. They didn't want Villas-Boas to realize how different they looked.

This line of speculation opens a series of interesting questions that eventually leads back to the Hills. The major problem with the Villas-Boas report is that he was alone. If the aliens' intention was producing a variety of humans, then they could only get halfway there with Villas-Boas, unless they had made other arrangements, or were interested in cloning.

The Hill abduction didn't suffer from that flaw. Like Villas-Boas, the Hill abduction seemed to be a target of opportunity. The Hills were driving along a virtually deserted stretch of highway. There were numerous side roads and very few inhabitants.The important aspect of the case, however, is the nature of the physical examinations. Both Barney and Betty reported things that are suggestive of sperm and egg extraction. The needle into Betty's navel was the easiest, least damaging route. Although Barney remembered nothing specific, there was the strange mark that he found on his groin.

The case can be made that the Hills reported a more scientific method of gathering the genetic material. Villas-Boas' abduction is more suggestive of experimentation in human psychology. At any rate, after the two abductions, the aliens certainly had all the genetic material they needed to produce humans in a variety of ethnic and racial types.

By the summer of 1962, the aliens could have produced several, live human babies, providing that they didn't have a method of speeding up the gestation. They may also have had a way of speeding up the maturing process.

This leads back to the October Scenario. The off-spring from the two abductions (and possibly several more that we don't know about) could have been as old as fifteen. By that age, conditioning by society would have had an influence, and should be having a greater part in the psychological formation. The aliens controlling the experiment wouldn't be able to produce the conditions for that formation without a wide range of knowledge. They may not have realized they needed it for the first several years of the experiment, and suddenly been confronted with a situation where they needed such information as fast as they could get it.

Anthropological studies involving rhesus monkeys have shown how quickly the mental state can collapse without the proper societal and psychological conditioning. Depriving the young of contact created individuals that were unable to function in society. When put into a larger group, the individuals ran to a corner to be alone and refused contact with the others. The aliens might have found themselves with a group of psychotic teenagers and had no psychological basis for action. They didn't know how to deal with the problem.

Building those kinds of files would explain the mental examinations reported by several of the October victims. Pat Roach, for example, claimed the aliens made her re-live experiences. They would need those kinds of things if they wanted to establish human qualities in their experimental children.It would also explain Pat Roach's statement that the aliens didn't understand how we (humans) are. They didn't understand our emotions. Because they didn't, they would need to learn about them quickly, especially if they had several psychotic teenaged boys and girls around.

This could also be reduced to the old argument about heredity and environment. The children produced by the aliens would have no environmental influences that would correspond to what they would expect on Earth, but they would have inherited the emotions of the humans. While certain behaviors are learned, there is no question that certain emotions begin to develop during puberty. A crisis of unknown proportions could develop for the alien experiment if they didn't acquire the knowledge to deal with the stresses being felt by the children.

And, because the human body also undergoes physical changes at that time, especially in girls, it would be something else they would have to learn about. A survey of their victims during the October Scenario suggests that they were looking for those answers. After all, the majority of the victims were female, from six year old Debbie Roach to nineteen year old Leigh Proctor to Pat Roach and Susan Ramstead. But, they also grabbed nineteen year old Calvin Parker and the middle aged Charles Hickson. They had nearly every stage of physical development for humans, except old age.

Suddenly in 1973, the aliens needed knowledge. They couldn't roam the skies for months covering their tracks. They had to have the knowledge so they elected to ignore caution, grab as many subjects as they could, and put them through examinations that would provide the information they needed. The mental and physical examinations showed this. At the same time, they had the opportunity to gather more genetic material. That would explain why several of the females remembered needles having been pressed into their navels.

So, in October 1973, the aliens returned with a mission. They were to gather as much data as possible about the human psychology and physiology. They needed to make their experiment with the human children work. They ignored caution in the name of haste. They left us with clues.

Of course, this might all be idle speculation. Science might be right. Villas-Boas might have been telling researchers his sexual fantasies. The Hills might have experienced some kind of a double hallucination. We might be right back where we started, with a group of aliens finding Earth for the fast time in 1973.But the question to ask here is, "What if the alternative is true?" Why would they want those children? Obviously, they could learn many things about the human mind from such an experiment. But why the sudden activity when the children would be teenagers? Why would they want to make them human?

This is where the theory breaks down. Not because it is built on a loose foundation, but because we don't have the information we need to add to the structure. We begin to use speculation in the place of facts, and the paths take us in a hundred directions without signs to lead us.

And, many of those paths are frightening. Aliens with a group of humans, real humans who are approaching thirty years of age. Humans that, if the information gained in 1973 was detailed enough that they could fit into our society without making a ripple. People who are humans, and yet they are not. Human in all outward appearances, and who, after October 1973, would be able to fit into society.

What their mission could be is anyone's guess. Maybe they plan to reveal themselves, that is, some kind of alien craft might land at the United Nations to announce to the world that they are here. Or maybe they are the spearhead for the invasion that the science fiction writers have predicted since H.G. Wells wrote THE WAR OF THE WORLDS.

Or, more likely, the children are an "anthropological" experiment, not unlike our primate centers. The aliens are studying for the sake of gaining knowledge.

That, in itself, is a horrible thought. A group of humans, now approaching thirty, living in a great, "natural habitat" while the aliens file by and look at the funny animals performing for them.

It's best to leave the alternative here, because we don't have the facts. There are facts to support the idea that the aliens returned to learn as much as they could about the human race. There are facts suggesting that the aliens were interested in human genetics and human psychology and it's not a big step to believe that the aliens had a use for the knowledge they gained. The new question is, "Why? Why do it at all?"

THE OCTOBER SCENARIO REVISITED

No theory is complete if it doesn't cover all the facts. Those theories that ignore part of the facts because they don't fit into the framework of the theory are flawed. With the October Scenario there is a body of information that is interesting but that has been ignored by me. Ignored because it doesn't fit with the October Scenario, but that does fit nicely into the alternative to the October Scenario.

In November 1957 there was a wave of UFO sightings in the southwestern United States. It was a time of low flying UFO's, many of them displaying for the first time, the electromagnetic effects. And it was a time when there were a large number of occupant reports. Occupant reports like the one given a few months later by Antonio Villas-Boas.

The briefest of surveys shows that the 1957 wave differed from all the others including October 1973, although the difference between them is slight. In 1957, we had many reports of stalled cars and burned people. After it, there were only occasional reports of electromagnetic effects and burned skin. But even that can fit into the pattern of the alternative to the October Scenario.

In Levelland, Texas, on November 2, Pedro Saucido was driving toward Levelland when a glowing UFO swept across the highway in front of his truck. As it landed nearby, the lights of the truck went out and the engine died. Saucido dived out the door and rolled out of the way. His passenger, Joe Salaz, sat terror-stricken, his eyes glued to the UFO. The blue-green glow faded into a red so bright that Salaz could no longer look directly at it.

During the three minutes that UFO sat on the highway, both men thought they heard noises coming from inside it. Suddenly the torpedo-shaped object, still glowing red, shot silently into the night sky.

Saucido was afraid to continue to Levelland because he thought that he might run into the object again. Instead he drove to another west Texas town and called the police in Levelland. A deputy listened to the report but laughed it off as, "another crazy flying saucer story."

About an hour later, Jim Wheeler saw a red, glowing UFO sitting on the road. As he neared it, his car engine died and the lights went out. The egg-shaped object then blasted off swiftly and silently. Wheeler's car started again and he called the Levelland police.

They had just finished talking to Wheeler when Jose Alvarez called to report that he had seen an egg-shaped object that killed his car engine. A few minutes later, Frank Williams walked into the sheriffs office.

James Long then called to say that he was driving on a county road northwest of Levelland when he came upon a landed, bright red UFO. His truck engine died and the lights went out. He got out and started toward the UFO, but it took off before he got more than a few feet from the truck. After the UFO was gone, his truck started easily.

Levelland Sheriff Weir Clem did not welcome the idea of chasing lights in the sky, and like his deputies, was inclined to laugh it off as more of those crazy flying saucer stories. Thunderstorms in the area were causing all the problems that he needed.

Just after midnight, Ronald Martin was nearing Levelland. He glanced at the dashboard amp meter, saw its needle jump to discharge then flip back as the engine died and the lights went out. He climbed out of his car to look under the hood, but found nothing wrong. As he turned, he saw the red UFO on the road. Unsure of what to do, Martin got into the car and tried to start it. After a few minutes, the UFO rose silently out of sight, and when it was gone, the car started.

After Martin's call, Clem decided to investigate and left the office with Patrick McCullough. About 1:30 a.m. they saw the glowing UFO streak by

160

them in the distance. About the same time, two highway patrol officers and Constable Lloyd Bonen saw the UFO. In all, five police officers saw the object, but none of them got close enough for the UFO to affect their car engines and lights.

Although there were many other sightings, including two at White Sands in the hours after Levelland, the next interesting case was reported on November 4 by James Stokes who was driving toward El Paso, Texas and was near Orogrande, New Mexico when his car's engine began to sputter and the radio faded out. As the engine finally died, Stokes guided his car to the side of the road. Ahead he could see a group of people talking and pointing to the sky. Looking up, he saw a large, oval-shaped object shooting toward the road. It buzzed the highway, turned to the northwest and then reversed for another pass at the cars before disappearing.

As the object passed over the cars, Stokes could feel its heat. He saw no portholes and thought that it was three thousand feet above the ground. Hours after he saw the UFO, Stokes noticed an itching on his face, hands and wrists. The areas that had been exposed to the UFO reddened as if they had been sunburned. Also on November 4 a large, orange object hovered briefly over Fort ,Itaipu, Brazil. Two sentries watched what they thought was a star as it became brighter and came closer. When it was close overhead, they felt something hot on their faces. One sentry dropped his rifle, started to run in panic, staggered and fell, unconscious. The other sentry screamed, awakening other men in the garrison.

Throughout the fort, men were running, confused. They turned on all the outside lights, and for a moment, everything was bright. Then the power failed, plunging the fort into darkness as the electrical systems collapsed.

One minute it was dark and the next it was light. The UFO took off, accelerating vertically. Some were in time to see it but most weren't. As the UFO disappeared, the lights came on. The two sentries were taken to the hospital for treatment for their burns.

On November 6, R.O. Schmidt walked into the Kearney, Nebraska, police station. He claimed that while he Was inspecting grain he found what he at first thought was a wrecked balloon. When he was thirty feet away he was stopped by a beam of light that paralyzed him.

Two aliens from the UFO, Schmidt now knew that it wasn't a balloon, searched him for weapons and then invited him on board. Inside he saw two women and three men working on instrumentation. He was told that no one meant him any harm. They wouldn't tell him where they were from but did say they might announce their presence to the world in the near future. When Schmidt left, there was a flash of light and the UFO was gone.

Police searched the area but could find no imprints, depressions or any burned vegetation. They did find a greenish, oil-like substance that they took to Kearney College for analysis. No one bothered to find out what it was after they took it to the college.

On November 6, Everett Clark saw a landed UFO In a field near his home in Dante, Tennessee, with four men and a woman. Clark talked to them briefly before they got into the UFO. It shot quietly into the sky.

Neighbors and friends described Clark as an intelligent and honest individual. They didn't think he would make up such a wild story. In the field they found that the grass had been depressed as if something very heavy had rested there. The Air Force didn't investigate. About an hour after Clark saw the landed UFO, several cars were stalled by another UFO near Santa Monica, California. Richard Kehoe was driving to work when the engine of his car died. Kehoe noticed that there were two other cars stalled, and when he got out, he could see a brightly lighted object on the beach.Kehoe and the men from the other cars, Ronald Burke and Joe Thomas, were talking when two humanoids got out of the egg-shaped UFO. and walked toward them. The creatures were yellowish-green in color and tried to talk to the terrified men. No one could understand them and fmally the aliens gave up. They returned to their craft and it took off.

When Clark first saw the UFO occupants, they had been trying to grab his dog. John Trasco of Everittstown, New Jersey claimed a brilliant egg-shaped object hovered over his barn. Underneath he saw a small, putty colored humanoid trying to grab his dog. Trasco yelled at the creature and it said that it only wanted the dog. Trasco told it to get the hell out of there and leave his dog alone. The alien dropped the animal and ran for the UFO. It took off straight up.

On November 7, Malvin Stevens was driving near Meridian, Mississippi, when he saw an object on the highway. As he approached, three men, four and a half feet tall, got out of it and came toward him. Stevens said that they wanted to talk, but he couldn't understand much of what they were saying. After several minutes, the creatures left and Stevens drove to Metfiphis to make a report.

On November 10, a Madison, Ohio woman said that she had been gardening when she saw a very bright triangle shaped UFO over her house. For thirty minutes she watched it but finally had to look away because it hurt her eyes. A few days later a rash developed over her body.

On the 14th, a hovering UFO flashed brightly, and the power in Tamaroa, Illinois failed. Power was out for ten minutes within a four-mile area.

After the fourteenth, there would be more reports but this marked the end of the wave as it is important to us. By December things had returned to normal. During the 1957 sightings, the Air Force received over a thousand reports. Like October 1973, it was a period of very intense activity that didn't fit the pattern of the other waves. Low level and landing craft, and reports of the creatures flying in them. And, those electromagnetic effects that stalled cars and doused lights.

Couple this with the Antonio Villas-Boas report and we have a very interesting bit of information. Assuming that the November 1957 wave was the first of the great UFO sightings, the first real reports after all the other noise has been filtered out, then we have our first clues.

Suppose that Villas-Boas was an experiment on reproduction as has been implied, overlooking that the genetics of such an attempt would render it almost impossible, then there should have been off-spring. Remembering that blood and tissue samples were taken and that each human cell contains the genetic code to reproduce the entire individual, the odds of off-spring are even greater. Then, sixteen years after Villas-Boas, when the off-spring would be fifteen or sixteen years old, the aliens return. They have a group of juveniles and they don't know how to handle them.

163

Emotionally, the children are causing them trouble. They must see how adults act, they must build a psychological profile, and they must build it quickly. So they return to look at the adults and compare them with the human children they have.

Or, it could be that once the aliens returned to their home world with all the human genetic material they had gathered, they realized that there was more information they needed. They then organized their return. Sixteen years later we had the rash of sightings of the October Scenario.

All this leads to one conclusion. We can expect the aliens to return sometime in the next two years. If the November 1957 sightings were the first prelude, as is logical after briefly looking at the data, then the October 1973 sightings were the second. That further implies that we may be in for the third set of sightings within the next couple of years.

And finally, if the October 1973 sightings marked the first real contact between our civilization and the aliens, we don't know when they will return. We don't have a time frame to put it into. We can only hope that it won't be the ten thousand years that Condon and all the others have postulated. And we can only hope that if they do return at that time, we won't be so busy trying to figure out that they're really here that we won't have time to make contact with them.

THE NATURE OF UFO RESEARCH

The major problem with the UFO phenomena is that there has been no consistency in the research. Some cases have been checked and re-checked while others that cry for additional research have been ignored. The men and women investigating the sightings range from the talented, thorough researcher to the totally inept bungler. They range from those who want answers to those who only want to add another case to their files. They range from the Air Force officer who was out to get all the information to the amateur who only wants to see his name in the paper.

When the Air Force or the Condon Committee was involved in UFO research, the major cases were covered. If a Pat Roach appeared during those years, someone with the credentials to study the case in depth with the money to follow up might have been dispatched. After 1969, the research was left to hobbyists. Many were good, searching long and hard for answers, but too many were sloppy.

Take, for example, my research into the Roach case. At the time the magazine gave me the assignment, I lived in Iowa. James A. Harder lived in California, and Pat Roach lived in Utah. We all spent a week in Utah, getting everything we could. I talked to the police, the neighbors and everyone else I could find. We spent days going over and over the sighting, and when we left, that was it.

But everyone who has read the report here knows that there are more questions to be asked. One question that's been posed, why in the hell didn't I interview the other boys who Debbie claimed that she had seen standing in the line?

Easy. Both of them were away from home for a couple of weeks, on some kind of religious camping trip. Of course, had I known at the time I was planning the trip that there were other witnesses, I could have asked if they would be available. But, I didn't learn about them until later.

Finally, I was back in Iowa writing my story. I called and talked to everyone again, but they had no additional conscious memories. I couldn't afford to return. I couldn't afford to have Harder return to complete the work., In fact, when I submitted the expenses, something less than five hundred dollars for the airfare, hotel and the dinner that I bought for everyone because Harder said the magazine could afford it, I was still asked why I had spent so much money. The magazine was interested in the story, as long as it didn't cost too much.

The same can be said about Susan Ramstead. There are more things to be done. There is that damned truck that she said was parked across the road. Susan couldn't see the license number, even under hypnosis, but there are things that could have been done to locate the driver. Access to the state's motor vehicle records would have helped. But since I wasn't a police officer and since I didn't have access to a hundred or more investigators, there is absolutely no way that I could find the driver.

Some time back, someone suggested NASA take over the investigation of UFO sightings. NASA politely declined the offer, saying that there was too much material out there that they wouldn't know where to begin. They would find themselves chasing down sighting reports that the Air Force had already investigated.

Actually, that's not true. The solution is to use the Air Force files, the Condon Committee's files, and everything else they could get such as the private files of the National Investigations Committee On Aerial Phenomena (NICAP), APRO, The Mutual UFO Network (MUFON), and anyone else who wanted to help, as a data base. They could index the books and magazines that have been devoted to the subject to build their data base, and then begin to study the new sightings as they came in.

Yes, it would be a Herculean task to assemble. Yes, it would take time and money, but then so does flights to the moon. In fact a small percentage of the money used for one space shot could finance the whole project. And then we'd have the people devoted to the problem who would be able to follow through on the investigations. Someone who could have gone back to Utah to interview the witnesses that I missed. Someone who could have gotten the state to cooperate with their files and who would have had the investigators to search for the driver of the other truck.

As it stands now, there is NO government investigation of UFO's. I have

166

heard that there is a Top Secret Air Force study, but know that there is not. Until July, 1986, I was a captain in the Air Force and through my job would have had to have access to the channels where those reports would have been made. There were no indications of that study and if there had been, I would have seen them.

The problem is that we are still busy arguing over the existence of UFO's. They do exist. They are something, whether it is a misinterpretation of natural phenomena or extraterrestrial spacecraft, it is time to end that debate. We must have a good, unbiased study of it. One that is searching for answers and that is not some kind of a PR operation whether for the government or for private individuals who are trying to earn money.

The last time there were visitations, we were so busy arguing about the existence of the UFO's that we made no attempt to expand the contact. It was a question of not seeing the forest because of all the trees.

Are there things to be done? Of course. There are so many UFO investigators and hobbyists and researchers out there, that the information is spread all over. Each is guarding his or her files for some unknown reason and each is unwilling to share those files with anyone else.

Not long ago I received a call from a fellow researcher who was angry about an occupant case that he had told me about. I had gotten a copy of his report, put a covering letter on it and forwarded it to APRO for their use. A few months later the report turned up in a book by Coral Lorenzen mentioning that it had been forwarded by me. He was mad that I would take HIS report and send it to SOMEONE ELSE.

My feeling is that all the information should be given to everyone. The only exceptions are those cases given in confidence. Some witnesses just don't need to be bothered by investigators searching for more information.

Everything that I have about Pat Roach, Susan Ramstead, Leigh Proctor and Dionisio Llanca is in the book. Granted, the files on them are much thicker, but a lot of that is preliminary information and adds nothing to the case. Rather than spending time going over old ground, new sightings, when they happen should be explored.

For all those who are interested, I would advise you to prepare for the next UFO wave. Don't worry about the past because those have been investigated. Look at the reports in this book. See the mistakes that I and the others made. No follow up investigations because there was no money to do them. Asking leading questions rather than just asking about what is happening. Missed bets. Witnesses who got away. Study that and then get ready for the next wave.

For those who are interested, I would advise the same thing that I said to NASA. Use the old material as a data base. Read it all. Study it and think about it. Ask yourself how you would have handled the investigation had you been there. Make notes and make plans so that you'll be ready.

And hurry. The next wave could start in the next few months. We'll be in the middle of it by next year. It's coming. All the signs point to it. Let's be ready for it.

AFTERWORD

The October Scenario is simply the theory that there have been no extra-terrestrial spacecraft in our atmosphere except for the brief period of October 1973. Prior to that time, there were misidentifications, hoaxes and lies. Afterward, there were more misidentifications and hoaxes. But in October 1973, the Earth received the once in ten thousand year visit that was postulated by Edward Condon and accepted as fact by dozens of scientists. They wouldn't accept daily visits claimed by millions of witnesses, but would admit a few highly isolated cases were possible.

The alternative to the October Scenario is also simple. It states that there may have been two other visits. These are the Hill case of 1961 and the 1957 wave that encompassed the Villas-Boas abduction. The purpose of these first visits was to gather genetic material to produce real humans. When the experiment ran into trouble several years later, the aliens found it necessary to visit Earth in October 1973 to gather data for psychological and physical profiles. Either of the two cases, including the 1957 wave, could be real, or both could, or neither. But they don't break the pattern established in 1973 and that is important.

Except for this brief period of activity, then, there have been no flying saucers. They were invented in the fertile imaginations of a hundred newspaper and magazine writers and kept alive by movies and books. The UFO field has been horribly over mined, overstated and over stressed.

The October Scenario doesn't preclude the possibly of other visits. In fact, it predicts them. And, it doesn't mean that there is only one group of aliens out there. Most scientists agree that the galaxy holds other intelligent life. And now that the ice has been broken by our visitors in 1973, we may expect more visits from other groups. Before Christopher Columbus there were very rare visits to North America by Europeans, but after him, the explorers arrived in droves. The same may happen to us now that the intelligences of other worlds know that we are here and that we have some semblance of civilization. (We can only hope that they don't mention the number of people who have tried to shoot the aliens the very first chance we get. Notice how many of the reports in October 1973 involve firearms.) All this is providing that these galactic races communicate with one another.

The point to remember. The October Scenario was real. It could happen again. It will happen again. And when it does, I hope that we are ready.

PHOTO APPENDIX

List of Illustrations

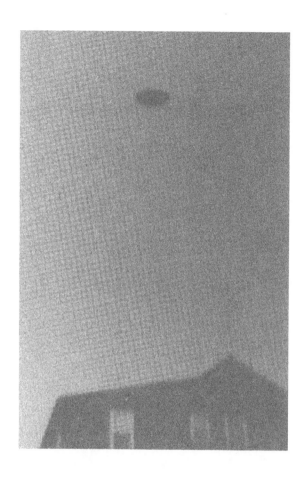

One of the first UFO pictures taken in the summer of 1947, it would become part of the noise that would conceal the October Scenario.

Above photo with background exposed to better accentuate the lights.

Salem, Massachussetts, 1953. The US Air Force explained away this sighting as a reflection off a window bu were unable to explain why the apparition was only there for three or four minutes and never reappeared.

Trinidad Island: This series of four photos, on this page and the next, taken off
the coast of Brazil dudring January, 1958

175

Examples of good photos but the story told by the witness is almost unbelievable.

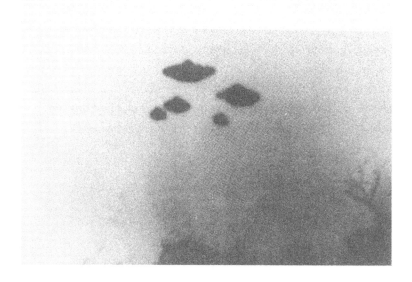

Light absorbing UFO seen in England. The photo is probably a fake, just more noise obscuring the facts.

The infamous Paul Villa photo created even more noise. Notice how in three photos on this page and the next, the object is always in perfect frame and evenly spaced between two trees. Using one of the tree branches as a reference point Air Force experts were able to calculate the size of the craft as about seven inches in diameter Obviously the US Air Force dubbed this one a fake.

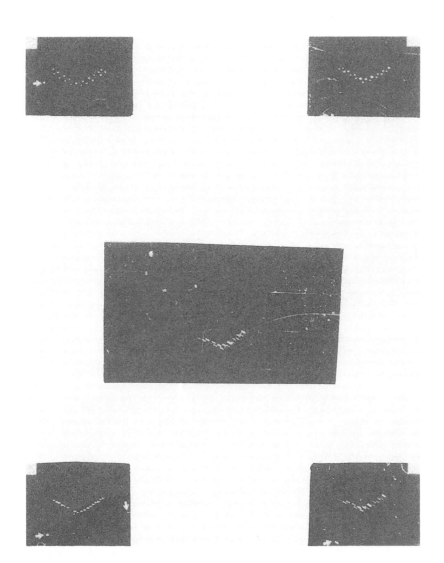

The **Lubbock Lights**: Again, there is so much controversy as to whether or not they are real that it became part of the background noise that obscured the real question.

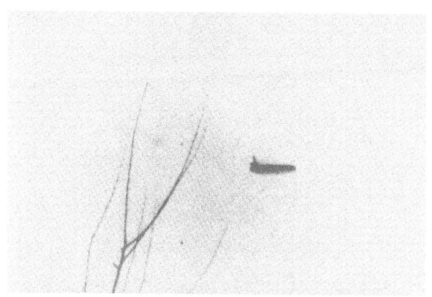

This photo was taken by teenage boys immediately subjecting its authenticity to scrutiny. An estimated 90 percent of all UFO photos have been taken by teenage boys and are fake.

Believe it or not this is photo of a 1935 Ford hubcap, taken near Riverside, California, in 1953.

Taken in South America, this is an example of a cigar-shaped craft, and ostensibly, a UFO leaving a trail. Its authenticity is open to question and contributes to the noise.

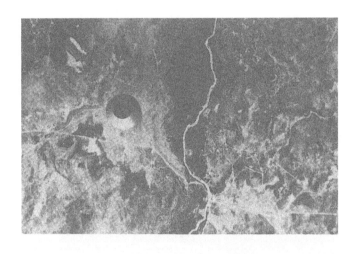

More noise. Both of the above photos were taken by Inake Oses of Venezuela. He later confessed that he had faked the images, his motive being revenge against the UFO community who had ridiculed him for not believing in UFOs. (Photos courtesy of APRO)

Ella Louise Fortune: Even though these three frames have been established as a lenticular cloud formation, twenty years later we are still enmired in an argument as to whether or not these are authentic UFOs.

This Brazilian photo has been studied by everyone under the sun including the US Air Force and the Condon Commission, who argued back and forth, discussing the shadows on the palms and they missed the point as to whether or not it was a UFO. Condon dubbed it a fake.

Before hypnosis this is how members of the Roach family remembered the aliens who invaded their home.

Pat Roach wanted to be sure we understood about the elongated eyes. She made this drawing to emphasize how different the eyes were.

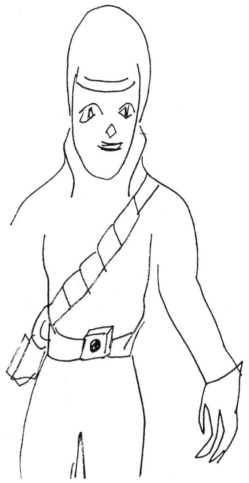

Under hypnosis we asked Pat Roach to draw the alien. Notice how this drawing differs from the one she drew while conscious.

After the first hypnosis session Pat drew the aliens as the remembered them. Notice how this one is a much more detailed drawing than the first simple sketch

The 1954 Occupant/Sightings Wave

Although the October Scenario focuses on the 1973 occupant sightings, there was another period of intense activity involving UFO occupants. This does not suggest the October Scenario is flawed, but in fact reinforces the theory. Coupling the October Scenario with the 1954 occupant sightings shows these two periods differ from every other UFO wave. Where most UFO sightings involved high flying craft, those of 1954 and 1973 featured ships on the ground and with the occupants outside of them.

The following pages include a partial list of the 1954 occupant sightings. It gives the flavor of the wave and points out the difference between it and the other waves (excluding 1973). Of further import, diligent study of these sightings suggests almost all other UFO sightings are part of the background noise.

Finally, the reason October of 1973 was identified as the one time of legitimate extraterrestial visits was because of the landed ships, the occupants reactions, and the actual contact between humans and the aliens. The only other time this happened was in 1954. This suggests that period of activity fits into the October Scenario pattern, and this is the point of UFO research: The search for patterns.

03/15/54 1700 Santa Maria, Brazil Rubem Hellwig Occupants Hellwig was driving when he spotted a football shaped object landing nearby. He stopped his car and approached the UFO. There were two creatures, about average size with brown faces and light hair. One was gathering samples while the other watched. They spoke to him in a language he couldn't understand. Finally they returned to their ship which took off, disappearing in the distance.

03/16/54 Santa Maria, Brazil Rubem Hellwig Occupants In his second sighting in two days, Hellwig came across the same ship the next day but with a different crew. There was a single man and two women. The women had long black hair, a dark complexion and large eyes. They told Hellwig that they were studying the natural riches of Brasil.

05/05/54 Goodland, KS Landing A farmer working his field came over a slight rise and saw a silver disc sitting on the ground. He watched as the legs retracted and it began to emit a loud whistling noise. It lifted up about a hundred feet, hovered there rocking gently and then one edge dipped and it vanished to the east.

05/11/54 Lawton, OK Occupant A lone man saw a disc shaped object hovering ten feet over the ground. Below it, in the shadow cast by it, he saw a single humanoid about four feet tall. When the creature saw the man there was a flash and the occupant was gone. A moment later the UFO took off to the west.

08/23/54 Thonon, France Occupants A man approached a landed UFO where two small creatures dressed in light color suits were standing. They grunted like pigs, entered the UFO which glowed brightly and then took off quickly.

09/10/54 Mourieras, France Occupants A farmer on his way home saw a man of average height who was wearing a helmet. The man made friendly gestures and finally turned, walking into the forest. A moment later a cigar-shaped craft lifted off.

09/10/54 Valenciennes, France Maruis Dewilde Occupants Dewilde was out at night, walking his dog along the railroad tracks when he spotted a dark mass sitting on it. Not far away were two creatures, small, with wide shoulders, wearing huge helmets. Dewilde planned to move on the men and delay them but a bright light from the craft paralyzed him. The creatures then returned to the craft and there was a loud whistling sound as the UFO rose into the sky. Later examination showed depressions on the ties where the object had stood.

09/15/54 Coldwater, KS Swain Occupants Swain, a twelve year old boy was returning home on his father's tractor when he saw a tiny man close by. The creature had a long nose and long ears. The creature seemed to fly over the ground and returned to a saucer shaped craft that opened up for him. It then glowed brightly and the object disappeared. The next day the sheriff found a set of triangle shaped marks in the field where the UFO had been.

09/17/54 Cenon, France Yves David Occupants David was bicycling when he felt a tingling all over his body. He stopped, got off and the light on his bike went out. In front of him he saw the dark shape of a machine about ten feet long and three feet high. David, the tingling having spread through his body and paralyzing him, watched as a small silhouette moved away from the machine. It approached him, touched him on the shoulder and then returned to its craft. The UFO gave off a greenish glow and disappeared. David recovered the use of his limbs then.

09/26/54 Valence, France Occupants A women, Leboeuf, had gone into the woods to gather mushrooms when she came across a small humanoid she thought was a scarecrow. It seemed to be wearing a diving suit with a clear helmet and when it came at her, she became frighted, fleeing. When she looked back, the creature was gone. A few moments later, there was a loud whistling and a disc shaped object rose from the woods. Evidence of its landing was later found.

09/30/54 Marcilly-sur-Vienne, France Occupants Eight construction workers saw a disc shaped object sitting on the ground. Nearby was a single, small humanoid wearing a helmet.

09/30/541845 Ligescourt, France Bernard Devoisin Occupants Devoisin and his friend Rene Coudette were riding their bicycles when they came across a glowing orange object sitting on the road. Near it was a small creature in a diving suit. It returned to the UFO which took off then.

10/04/54 2000 Poncey, France Yvette Fourneret Landing As she was about to close the window, she saw a small object ten feet in diameter hovering near a plum tree. The glow of the object threw a pale light on the tree. Fourneret ran next door and moments later two men, armed with shotguns entered the field. They didn't find the UFO but did find a hole where it looked as if the soil had been pulled from the ground.

10/04/54 Salta, Argentina Occupants A number of children came across three small creatures that had greenish skin. They resembled humans vaguely.

10/05/54 Loctudy, France Occupants A baker was drawing water from a well when he noticed an object, ten feet in diameter sitting on the ground. A small being with a hairy face and large, oval eyes approached. It talked to him in a strange language. The baker called his boss and they watched the creature get back into the craft which then took off quickly.

10/05/54 Mertrud, France Occupants A road repairman spotted a strange object sitting on the road. Near it was a small, hairy creature which returned to the craft and it took off. Traces from the craft were found on the road.

10/09/54 Pournoy, France Occupants Four children saw a bright glow from a nearby cemetery. Approaching, they saw a small object, eight feet in diameter standing on three legs. A small creature with a bright light in its hand came out. It was hairy and had large eyes. The creature talked to them but they couldn't understand it. They ran away and when they looked back, the UFO was in the sky, flying away.

10/09/54 Carcassonne, France Jean Bertrand Occupants Bertrand was driving when he spotted a spherical object sitting on the road in front of him. Through a translucent top, he could see a human shaped shadow moving. As he approached, the object took off.

10/09/54 Rinkerode, Germany Occupants A projectionist saw a cigar shaped craft giving off a blue light sitting near the road. Near the object were four small beings wearing rubber overalls and who seemed to be working on the underside of the object. The creatures had large chests and thin arms and legs.

10/09/54 Lovoux, France Occupants A man bicycling saw a small creature with a double beamed light in his hand. The being used the light to paralyze the man. It walked along the road and then disappeared into the forest.

10/11/54 Taupignac, France Occupants Three men traveling in a car spotted a disc shaped craft sitting in a field. Near it were four tiny humanoids working. When they saw the men, they ran to the disc, shooting a beam of light at the men so that they couldn't give chase. The UFO then took off.

10/11/54 0400 La Croix Durade, France Landing Traces A glowing object was seen lifting from a field. It disappeared from sight in seconds and leaving flattened grass and other traces behind.

10/12/54 Teheran, Iran Occupants A disc shaped object was seen hovering close to the ground. The witness reported that he could clearly see a being inside, moving around. It was tiny and dressed in black. When a crowd began to gather, the UFO flew off.

10/12/54 Pt. Lauttey, Morocco Occupants A French engineer saw a small man, about four feet tall, dressed in a silver suit entering a disc shaped object. It took off quickly, disappearing in seconds.

10/13/54 Bourasote, France Occupants Three people saw a reddish colored disc about twelve feet in diameter. Although the three witnesses were not together, they all reported the being wore a shiny suit, had a large head and enormous eyes. The man closest to the UFO claimed he was paralyzed and when the object took off, he was thrown to the ground.

10/14/54 Meral, France Occupants A farmer was getting ready to leave his house when a glowing ball landed not far away. It gave off a bright light that illuminated the fields for about two hundred yards around it. As he approached it, he saw a domed disc that appeared to be translucent and behind the glow he could see a dark shape moving. The color then changed from white to red and the object took off at great speed.

10/15/54 Toulouse, France Occupants The witness reported that he saw a small creature with large eyes near a small disc shaped craft.

10/16/54 Baillolet, France Dr. Henri Robert Occupants Robert watched four disc shaped objects fly over. One of them dropped out of the formation and as it approached the ground Robert's car stalled and the lights went out. Robert felt as if he was paralyzed and sat in the car during the whole sighting. A small creature appeared and moved, illuminated by the glow from the UFO. When the light went out, he could see nothing. Finally the UFO took off and Robert could again move and his car started again.

10/17/54 Corbierres Occupants A man walking in the forest came upon a landed disc shaped craft. He spotted the helmeted occupants and turned to run. His dog approached and then retreated, walking in a strange manner.

10/17/54 Isle of Capri Occupant An artist taking a walk came upon a landed disc shaped craft about fifteen feet in diameter. Four small creatures dressed in coveralls came out of it.

10/18/54 Doubs, France Occupants A women riding a motorcycle came to an area where there was a red glow on the road. She thought nothing of it and moments later saw a figure by the side of the road. It was dressed in a one piece silver suit accompanied by two smaller beings. She continued on and looked back in time to see a round object lifting into the sky.

10/18/54 2040 Fontenay-Forey, France Occupants A man and his wife watched a cigar shaped craft as it suddenly dived toward the ground. The couple approached it and saw a small being about three feet tall. The eyes seemed to glow orange. Four others reported watching the red glowing cigar in flight.

10/18/54 2100 Royan, France Occupants A couple watched two ball shaped UFO's joined by a bright beam of light. The light went out and the two balls landed separately. A creature, small got out of each object, passed each other and entered the opposite object. The UFO's then took off and flew off.

10/21/54 1645 Shrewsbury, England Jennie Roestenburg Occupants Roestenburg said that she and her two children watched an aluminum colored disc with transparent panels. Inside they could see two men with white skin and long hair. They wore skin tight suits and helmets.

10/27/54 Les Jonquets-de-Livet, France Occupants A farmer watched a cigar shaped object with lights on each end land in a nearby field. He didn't investigate then, but later, when a motorcyclist fell, he and a group of people sighted the object. Two small creatures in silver suits were seen near it. The UFO took off silently.

11/02/54 Santo Amaro, Brazil Occupants A taxi driver saw a large, glowing object sitting in a vacant field between two houses. As he approached, a door opened in the side and he entered. Inside, he saw a table with maps on it, including one of South America. While he was studying the map, three creatures, perfectly formed humans, but much smaller appeared. Although they made no move toward him, he found himself backing out of the craft, almost against his will. Once he was outside, the UFO took off.

11/08/54 Monza, Italy Occupants A huge crowd went to investigate a light and saw three creatures near a disc shaped object sitting on three legs. The beings spoke with gutteral sounds. The creatures got into their ship and it lifted without a sound.

11/14/54 Isola, Italy Occupants A farmer watched a cigar shaped object land in a field and three small beings got out. Convinced that they were going to steal his rabbits, he ran for his rifle, but when he aimed it, it grew heavy and he dropped it. Then he became paralyzed. The beings took the rabbits and returned to their ship. When it lifted silently, the farmer could move again. He picked up his rifle and fired it once at the ship.

11/14/54 0330 Brazil Occupants A railroad employee spotted three small humanoids who seemed to be examining the railroad bed with a lantern. They wore tight fitting, luminous clothes. When they saw the employee, they ran back to their ship, an oval shaped object, which rose straight into the sky and disappeared quickly.

11/28/54 0200 Caracas, Venezuela Gustavo Gonzales Occupants Gonzales and his friend Jose Ponce were driving toward a produce warehouse when they sighted a glowing sphere hovering just above the street. Gonzales got out and spotted a small, hairy creature with glowing eyes. Gonzales tried to grab the creature which struck him, knocking him backwards. The being then advanced, clawed hands extended and Gonzales pulled his knife. He struck the creature in the shoulder, but the blade glanced off. Another being came from the ship and both returned to it. The UFO took off swiftly.

12/04/54 Pontal, Brazil Jose Alves Occupants Alves watched a disc shaped object land and three small men, dressed in tight fitting clothes got out. They gathered samples of the plants and one got some water from a nearby stream. They then returned to their craft and it took off swiftly.

12/09/54 Linha Bela Vista, Brazil Occupants A farmer working in his fields heard a sound like a sewing machine and looked up to see a disc shaped object hovering. The animals in the field under it scattered. Three men of medium height were visible. One stayed in the craft looking out a hatch while the others came forward. The fanner dropped his hoe and one of the beings picked it up and handed it back. It then pulled up some of the plants. The farmer spoke to the creatures but they didn't seem to understand. They returned to their craft and it took off.

12/10/54 Caracas, Venezuela Occupants Two men watched two small men run into the bush. A few minutes later a glowing, disc shaped object rose into the sky with a si7Jling sound.

12/10/54 Chico, Venezuela Occupants Two boys, while out hunting spotted a shiny object they described as two soup bowls put together. Four small, hairy creatures came from it and tried to drag one of the boys toward it. The other struck the creatures but the shotgun bounced off. The struggle ended and the creatures returned to their craft. Investigators taken to the site found physical evidence of a struggle.

12/11/54 Linha Bela Vista, Brazil Occupants A farmer went out to investigate a noise when he saw a object, squared, with a bottom like that of a tea kettle hovering over a field. He saw two humanoids in the field. The fanner started toward them but they tried to warn him off. When he refused to stop, they pulled up a tobacco plant and ran to their craft.

312/15/54 Campo Grande, Brazil Occupants A man who was fishing sighted two objects hovering overhead, one revolving around the other.

Using the telescopic sight on his rifle he watched as three creatures desended, gathered samples and then returned to their craft.

12/16/54 San Carlos, Venezuela Occupants Three men returning home, stopped along the side of the road. Jesus Paz got out and walked into the bushes. A moment later he screamed and his friends ran to his aid. They found him on the ground and a short, hairy creature running away. A flat, shiny object then rose into the sky, disappearing in seconds.

12/19/54 Valencia, Venezuela Occupants A jockey, running in the cool early morning, came across a disc-shaped craft hovering just off the ground. Several small creatures were loading boulders into the craft. When they spotted the jockey, they turned some kind of device on him that emitted a purple light that paralyzed him. The creatures returned to their craft and it took off. Later investigations showed strange tracks on the ground.

Glossary

Abduction—is the idea that creatures from the spacecraft took people on board for the purpose of examination and experimentation. The experience was not a pleasant event since it was involuntary. See Contactee.

Airship—refers to the Great Airship allegedly seen over the United States in 1897.

Ancient Astronauts—the theory that beings from outer space landed on Earth in the distant past, and helped to construct the civilizations that flourished then.

APRO—Aerial Phenomena Research Organization. The first of the civilian groups devoted to the study of UFO's and founded by Jim and Coral Lorenzen

Condon Committee—the scientific study made by the University of Colorado and headed by Doctor Edward U. Condon. The Air Force sponsored the study and its results were released in 1969.

Contactee—A person who claims to have met the benevolent space brethren, took rides on their craft to other planets and who later claimed to have a message for all of the human race. They never offered any proof for their stories. See Abductions.

Earthquake Lights—A natural phenomenon caused by the stressed along earthquake faults. The displays are luminous, spin and have been described as saucer shaped.

Electromagnetic Effects—Also called EM Effects. This is the effects of the electromagnetic fields on electrical devices on the ground. EM Effects have been responsible for stalling car engines, dimming the lights, and blacking out some communities.

Extraterrestrial—Anything or anyone who comes from anywhere but the Earth. Meteors and comets have extraterrestrial origins.

Hypnotic Regression—The taking of a person back to a specific experience with hypnosis with the hope of gaining a clearer idea of how an event transpired. In UFO research, it is often the only method of learning about Abduction.

NICAP—National Investigations Committee on Aerial Phenomena. A civilian organization based in Washington DC and that was quite vocal in the research of UFO's.

Occupants—The creature or being the ride in the flying saucers.

Occupant reports - Are those cases where the beings in the UFO was seen.

Ockham's Razor—is the principle that the simplest solution is probably the correct one. Why postulate complications to cases when they are not necessary?

Oopth's—Also called Out of Place Artifacts. These are items found in places they don't belong such as a silver serving bowl found in stone. The suggestion is that such artifacts demonstrate an ancient history millions of years old.

Polygraph—Also called a lie detector. It is sometimes employed in UFO cases to determine whether or not the witness believes the story he or she is spinning.

Project Bluebook—the official Air Force investigation of Unidentified flying Objects that was ended in 1969 after the results of the Condon Committee were released.

Project Grudge—The official Air Force investigation of Flying Discs that followed Project Sign and preceded Project Bluebook.

Project Sign—The first of the studies of the Flying Discs, started in 1947 after the Kenneth Arnold sighting.

Time Discrepancy—The difference in a UFO sighting of the time the witness thinks it lasts and the actual length of time that passes. A big discrepancy is one of the red flags of an abduction case.
UFO—Unidentified Flying Object or a flying saucer. An Extraterrestrial spaceship.

Zeta 1 Reticuli—Part of the double star system with Zeta 2 Recticuli. According to the Hill Star Map, it is the place where the aliens live. It is about 38 light years from the Earth.

Index

What To Do If You Sight An Unidentified Flying Object

One of the questions asked most often is where can I report my UFO sighting? The U.S. Air Force recommends calling a local university. The local police will sometimes investigate, but then the information is then filed and often forgotten. If there is a local UFO organization, they might offer a few ideas. But the problem with all of the aforementioned is that your UFO sighting could easily be lost in the shuffle of paperwork. Ironically, it may be the single sighting everyone could benefit from.

So, if you see a UFO the best place to report it is:

The J. Allen Hynek Center for UFO Studies
P.O. Box 31335
2457 West Peterson Avenue
Chicago Illinois 60659

Or call twenty-four hours a day (312) 271-3611.

An experienced researcher will investigate your sighting and provide information about it. They will try to answer your questions. All sighting reports remain confidential.

About The Author

Born in Cheyenne, Wyoming in 1949, Captain Kevin D. Randle served as an Army helicopter pilot in Vietnam where he was awarded the Silver Star, The Distinguished Flying Cross as well as a number of other decorations. Later, he served as an intelligence officer in the USAF.

A field investigator for APRO, Randle has studied UFO phenomena since 1965. He began his writing career by publishing numerous articles in UFO Report, Official UFO, Saga, True, and Argosy magazines. He is also well known for his series of novels Vietnam Ground Zero authored under the pen name of Eric Helm. He and his wife Debbie make their home in Cedar Rapids, Iowa.

CPSIA information can be obtained
at www.ICGtesting.com
Printed in the USA
BVHW041310270122
627380BV00014B/215

9 780934 523356